HELLENISTIC
ASTROLOGY
FOR BEGINNERS

An Introduction to the Origins
and Practice of Predictive Astrology

HELLENISTIC
ASTROLOGY
FOR BEGINNERS

Malorine Mathurin

ROCKRIDGE
PRESS

For general information on our other products and services or to obtain technical support, please contact our Customer Care Department within the United States at (866) 744-2665, or outside the United States at (510) 253-0500.

Rockridge Press publishes its books in a variety of electronic and print formats. Some content that appears in print may not be available in electronic books, and vice versa.

Interior and Cover Designer: Jay Dea
Art Producer: Samantha Ulban
Editor: John Makowski
Production Editor: Rachel Taenzler

Illustrations © Brigantine Designs/Creative Market, Cover, p.22; J. Oliver Designs/Creative Market, pp. ii, vii, iix, 20, 48, 54, 56, 68, 69 72, 92, 94, 106, 124, Classic Collection/Alamy Stock Photo p.34. All other illustrations used under licence Shutterstock. Author Photo Courtesy of Markus Winter.

ISBN: Print 978-1-64739-691-6 | eBook 978-1-64739-424-0
R0

This book is dedicated
to my family
and friends, who supported
my intense connection to
and obsession with astrology
and the cosmos.

CONTENTS

INTRODUCTION

Mankind has always been intrigued by the planets, the constellations, and the stars that surround our world. The exploration of who we are and the development of a system to understand our place within the cosmos are important facets of the human experience. For more than two thousand years, human beings have striven to understand the groupings of infinite celestial bodies, planets, stars, and moons as seen from Earth.

Our ancestors looked to the sky for guidance, direction, and answers to life's questions, such as "Who am I?" and "What is my purpose?" as well as answers to questions for the everyday, such as "When will rain fall for my crops?" Astrology and astronomy simultaneously tried to answer these questions. Astrology, according to the *Oxford English Dictionary*, is "the study of the movements and relative positions of celestial bodies interpreted as having an influence on human affairs and the natural world."

Astrology has played a large role in shaping my academic journey. As a bookish child, if someone mentioned killer whales I went straight to the *Encyclopædia Britannica* to see what they looked like, what they ate, and how they moved. If a reference was made to a historic building, I went directly to the library's microfilm department to learn more. My great-grandmother, who hailed from the island of Trinidad, gifted me my first Rider-Waite tarot card deck when I was seven years old. I did not know what the cards were but was utterly fascinated by the artwork and the figures in the scenes, and I was determined to find out what they meant. In doing this research, I noticed that both astrology and numerology played a part in understanding the cards. My obsession with astrology had begun.

Soon I had read every book in the library related to modern-day astrology, written by the likes of Donna Cunningham, Noel Tyl, Jan Spiller, Liz Greene, Robert Hand, and Linda Goodman, to name a few. Then I moved on to the classic astrologers: Johannes Kepler, Nicolaus Copernicus, and Claudius Ptolemy. This is where I found Hellenistic astrology, which answered questions that many modern astrologers neglected to discuss. As these gaps were filled, I fell in love with the ancient science of Hellenistic astrology.

I studied fine art and painting as an undergraduate and later earned both a master's degree in art history and a master of philosophy degree in anthropology. Employed as a cultural anthropologist in the UK, I always referred back to astrology, my first love. Returning to the States, I taught classes on astrology, divination, and tarot.

In this book, we will create a bridge from early Hellenistic astrology to modern astrology, leading you to a deeper understanding of the concepts and techniques of this ancient science.

CHAPTER 1

The Story behind Hellenistic Astrology

In this chapter, we will explore the definition and origins of Hellenistic astrology. Although the origins of this system are shrouded in mystery, we shall consider several archaeological clues that indicate a number of ancient civilizations created tales, myths, and folklore to explain the movements and interactions of the Earth, the Moon, the planets, and the stars.

Understanding the cosmos began with the simple observation of the changing planetary positions and corresponding natural happenings occurring within human memory. These planetary occurrences were recorded with the intention of determining patterns and theories of everyday events. Ancient Babylonians and Mesopotamians divided the zodiac into sects and houses, which made analysis manageable. Babylonian researchers based their cosmology on the idea that the Earth was a living entity orbited by the surrounding planets and stars. This concept was carried through the evolution of astrology as one way to understand Earth and our place in the cosmos, providing nourishment for the beginning of Hellenistic astrology.

What Is Hellenistic Astrology?

Astrology has played a role in every large ancient civilization, from the Egyptians to the Babylonians to the Maya. The practice of Hellenistic astrology specifically has had a huge influence on astrology around the globe, including Indian, Arabian, European, and Western astrology. Hellenistic astrology is considered to have been the first system with the structure and theory of modern astrology and is aptly deemed the "Grandfather of Astrology." Although the exact dates of the development of Hellenistic astrology are unknown, it's said to have developed in the Mediterranean region (namely Greece, Persia, and Egypt) between the death of Alexander the Great in 323 BCE and the emergence of the Roman Empire in 31 BCE, also known as the Hellenistic period. The name "Hellenistic" comes from the word *Hellas*, the ancient name for Greece, and the Hellenistic period was the golden age of Greek art, culture, philosophy, and science.

In its most basic form, Hellenistic astrology is a system of horoscopic astrology, which uses the Ascendant—the first impression or "face" of an individual, situation, or event—as the beginning point of astrological practice. The term "horoscope" is derived from the ancient Greek term *hōroskopos*, which means "hour-marker," and is used to denote the Ascendant as the first house (or the first "pie section") of the astrological birth chart. In modern times, the term "horoscope" is usually used to indicate an overview of the daily occurrences affecting each astrological sign, but originally it referred to a chart—known today as a "natal chart" or "birth chart." Birth charts are a snapshot of the planetary positions at the exact time of an individual's birth.

Many well-known ancient Greek and Egyptian philosophers wrote about the theories and practices of Hellenistic astrology. The first sets of data were compiled around the second century BCE by the Egyptian pharaoh Nechespo and his aide and high priest, Petosiris. Four general treatises of astrology survive; the most notable book is *Tetrabiblos: Or the Quadripartite Mathematical*

Treatise, written by Claudius Ptolemy in the second century CE. Vettius Valens wrote *Anthology*; Hephaestion of Thebes wrote the *Apotelesmatics*; and Firmicus Maternus wrote *Mathesis, or Ancient Astrology: Theory and Practice*. A fifth writing, *Carmen Astrologicum*, by Dorotheus of Sidon, is composed of fragmented, didactic verse on astrology. It is considered one of the stronger, more traditional sources of information on Hellenistic astrology.

Branches of Hellenistic Astrology

Three different branches of astrology developed within ancient Greece: natal astrology, universal astrology, and katarchic (or inceptional) astrology.

NATAL ASTROLOGY

Natal astrology is also known as genethlialogy, which derives from the Greek word *genethlios*, meaning "pertaining to one's birth" or "the study of nativities." This first branch is closest to what we call modern astrology. According to astrologer Chris Brennan, genethlialogy is "the practice of studying the positions of the planets at the moment of a person's birth in order to determine information about the nature and course of their life." The birth chart, or *thema*, represents the blueprint of an individual's soul journey. Natal astrology was guided by the Greco-Roman focus on individuation, rather than on the livelihood of the community or of a group of people.

During this time period, only someone of importance, like a king, politician, or priest, used astrology in their everyday life. Nowadays, natal astrology focuses on the birth chart of any individual. Many people use the analysis of their birth chart to understand their life's direction and purpose, the best ways to overcome hardships or conditioned responses from their past or childhood, and what to look forward to in the future.

One of the benefits of natal astrology is the ability to use rectification, a method to create a birth chart when the client does not know their exact birth time or when the time was not recorded on their birth certificate. A birth chart can be rectified using any event that has occurred in the past, such as the birth of a child, a marriage, or the change of structure in government—this will all be reflected in natal astrology with almost perfect accuracy. Recording important events can establish patterns, which helps individuals plan their lives according to the key dates of previous occurrences—for example, Mondays are always good for weddings, or June 1 is the best day to apply for a job.

The use of an ephemeris—a table or list of data with pre-calculated positions of celestial bodies—is helpful when rectifying a chart. Once an important event is chosen, one would be able to procure a birth chart reading by using these predetermined calculations. The ephemeris is crucial in understanding the placements on an astrological chart.

UNIVERSAL ASTROLOGY

Universal astrology derives its name from the ancient Greek word *katholikos*, meaning "concerning the whole," "general," or "universal." Universal astrology was more closely linked to the way astrology was utilized in the Babylonian and Mesopotamian eras, which was to track natural phenomena, such as tornadoes or rainstorms. Records of these celestial events are found in the Enuma Anu Enlil, a series of clay tablets. Astrologers and star-gazers recorded and tracked the appearance of the Moon and its "horns"; the month and day of its transitions; its magnitude; and the duration, color, and direction of lunar and solar eclipses. They also recorded the direction and intensity of the blowing wind and the connection to the Moon's movements with rain, lightning, thunder, earthquakes, mudslides, and clouds. Universal astrologers kept track of these phenomena to maintain a log of when natural events occurred and the country, city, or people to be forewarned.

Universal astrology also determined good or bad omens that might affect entire kingdoms or the royal family. Babylonian and Mesopotamian royalty were viewed as those "chosen" to rule by divine right and were therefore seen to be closer to the heavens, like gods. Historian David Edwin Pingree notes that "the importance of celestial omens in Mesopotamian royal courts from the last few centuries of the 2nd millennium BC till the Achaemenid period depended on their being regarded as the principle means for the gods to signal their intentions to the king. [The royal courts] employed numerous observers to watch the heavens for the divine messages." These royal astrologers became adept at observing changes in the celestial sphere and at devising elaborate, sophisticated mathematical techniques and structures to track and monitor these changes. This led to the development of mathematical astronomy, which became a form of science in and of itself.

KATARCHIC ASTROLOGY

Katarchic or inceptional astrology is named from *katarche*, an ancient Greek word meaning "inception," or the start. Katarchic astrology is similar to electional astrology, in which the astrologer uses a client's series of dates to determine the quality or auspiciousness of a certain event or occurrence. This branch combines the branches of natal and universal astrology in that the astrologer will cast a "birth" chart for the potential beginning of an event or happening, such as a marriage, the start of a new job, or the founding of a new company or city. This information can help pinpoint the best dates to conduct these activities. For instance, if someone were able to tell you the best time to sit for a job interview, you would most likely follow their advice. In Hellenistic astrology, the astrologer can determine the beginning of a venture or event or the best dates to partake in said event (*katarche*) as well as the potential (*apotelesma*) of the desired development.

What Is the Relationship between Hellenistic Astrology and Western Astrology?

Western astrology is derived from Hellenistic astrology. There are many similarities, but as the latter was practiced over two thousand years ago, there are of course a few differences. Western astrology primarily utilizes natal astrology, which underpins the majority of conversations about astrology and planetary influences in popular culture. People use natal charts to learn more about themselves and their environments in order to make the necessary changes to attain their life purpose (or North Node). Universal astrology is still used when studying the astrology of a city, country, or event, and katarchic astrology is also widely used to determine appropriate dates and times to relocate, start a new job, or get married. Many new branches of astrology build on the *katarche* method, such as astrocartography, which maps out what new location will be most auspicious for your life goals or soul purpose.

Another addition to the world of astrology since Hellenistic times is the use of transits, or secondary or progressed chart readings, which can determine how the planets and signs have shifted in your chart since the time of your birth, making for a new evaluation of life goals and purpose. Hellenistic astrologers called these techniques "annual profections" (see page 109) and "zodiacal releasing" (see page 116). As the Hellenistic methods involved quite a bit of math and complicated formulas, many modern astrologers do not use these techniques and prefer to use transit charts instead.

For instance, if someone had their North Node, or life purpose, in Aries in their birth chart and it since transitioned into Pisces, this would mean a huge shift in purpose for the individual. This indicates a move from focusing on developing assertiveness and individuality to helping the wider society or diving deeper into spiritual or creative work—a major change in direction for anyone.

Historical Origins and Contemporary Revival

To thoroughly understand the meaning and relationship of astrological concepts, we need a deeper understanding of the origins of
Hellenistic astrology. Ancient Greek philosophers maintained that
Hellenistic astrology originated in Greece. However, as we shall see,
there were influences from other cultural groups—including the
Mesopotamians, Egyptians, and, later, the Romans—that shaped
its development.

MESOPOTAMIAN ASTROLOGY

As Professor Beverley Milton-Edwards notes, Mesopotamia
"inspired some of the most important developments in human
history including the invention of the wheel, the planting of the
first cereal crops, and the development of cursive script." Those
living in what we now refer to as the cradle of civilization developed
philosophies, mathematical techniques, astronomy, astrology, and
divination. Divination is found in all ancient and modern human
societies, but consulting the will of the gods was especially important in Mesopotamia. Divination underlaid almost every political,
social, or private undertaking. The holistic Mesopotamian world-
view held that all objects and events in the Universe operated from
a place of divine will.

Mesopotamia had four main classifications of divination: artificial, inspired, deductive, and natural. Dr. Ulla Koch-Westenholz
defines "natural divination" as a more direct form of communication from the gods, relayed through oracles or in dreams (where "the
mind seizes from without"), whereas "artificial divination" required
information to be observed and studied to determine the will of the
gods. For example, artificial divination can be seen in the recording of the seasons, which created a calendar to mark when the sun
would fall below the horizon for six months, creating less daylight,

and when it would stay longer above the horizon, giving more hours of daylight.

"Inspired divination" consisted of symbols and messages from the gods in their effort to connect with or warn humans. "Deductive divination" included omens that are manifested only through ritual, like extispicy, the reading of anomalies in animal entrails, and lecanomancy or scrying, the reading of shapes or symbols created when adding flour or oil to water.

One example of deductive divination concerns Alexander the Great. According to Arrian of Nicomedia, Peithagoras the diviner told Alexander not to be afraid of the king Hephaestion while traveling toward Babylon. Peithagoras "derived his knowledge of the future from the inspection of the inward parts of animals." In this, he twice found a growth or lobe in the liver of the sacrificial animal, which meant that the king would soon be dead—and the king did die a day after the prediction. All forms of divination work well together. For instance, ominous signs can be seen within astrology, and natural divination can foretell astrological or astronomical events.

An example of natural divination is seen in the *Anabasis of Alexander*, a history of the campaigns of Alexander the Great written in the second century CE by Arrian of Nicomedia. Alexander ignored warnings from Chaldean philosophers who instructed him not to enter the city of Babylon at the end of his longstanding reign in Asia, Europe, and Africa. The Chaldeans, or "nativity-casters," a group of Mesopotamian priests who specialized in divination, astrology, and mathematics, received "oracular declaration" from the god Belus to warn Alexander of his impending death.

The Chaldeans casted nativities, or natal charts, to forecast planetary changes and shifts in what was happening in society. The Chaldeans can be connected to the biblical Magi or Wise Men in the Gospel of Matthew. This group of astrologers traveled from the East (most likely Persia or Mesopotamia) to bring gifts to the infant Jesus before his birth. They were guided by a prophet who told them to follow a star to Bethlehem to find the child of God. According to the ancient Greek historian Diodorus Siculus, the Chaldeans were seen to "practice and observe the star of Arabia and the marvels of that land." There is evidence that the Chaldeans are viewed as some of the original astrologers or prophets, although Diodorus notes that the Mesopotamians might actually have learned astrology from the Egyptians.

Divination was an important feature of astrology and astronomy. Astrology in the Hellenistic period was tied to reading and interpreting predictive omens, called "heavenly writing" or "heavenly scripts to be read and interpreted." Astrology was the language the gods used to deliver messages and intentions to mankind.

Ancient Babylonian astrologers believed that the world was a tablet and the gods inscribed these heavenly messages into the sky. In the Neo-Assyrian era, "colleges," or elite groups of literate scholars and astrologers, served the royal kingdom by sending reports and letters of predictions for the continued functioning of the country, city, or kingdom. Trained astrologers maintained this "scribal tradition" by recording the celestial omens collected over the years. These large libraries of heavenly writing were kept in compiled cuneiforms or large stone or clay tablets, the most well-known of which is the Enuma Anu Enlil.

Astrological observations were recorded in the Astronomical Diaries, or simply the Diaries, which the Akkadian Empire referred to as *naṣāru ša ginê*, or "regular watching." Astrologers observed natural occurrences, like eclipses, sunsets, and the phases of the Moon, and recorded them in the Diaries.

Natal astrology became popular in the fifth century BCE as Mesopotamian astrologers began using "the seven wandering stars" or planets (see page 21) in addition to the monthly zodiacal signs to create individualized birth charts. The interpretations of these charts were based on the qualities of the sign, planet, and placement to determine collective personality traits, future events in the individual's life, and the people they may attract.

For instance, one translated Babylonian birth chart in the *Babylonian Horoscopes* determined:

> 2 **He will be lacking property, ...**
> 3 **His food will not [suffice] for his hunger.**
> 4 **The property which he had acquired in his youth will not last.**
> 5 **The 36th year he will have property.**

Artificial, inspired, deductive, and natural divination were part of the understanding of Hellenistic astrologers as they began the first instance of divining by entities that were not human. These divinations connected us to information that could not be understood by fact alone. Egypt had many similar connections to divination and astrology.

EGYPTIAN ASTROLOGY

Ancient Egyptians contributed to modern astrology by combining astronomy, record timing, and the study of mathematics with the divination practices of Babylonian and Mesopotamian astrology. Similar to Mesopotamian astrology, ancient Egyptian astrology operated on a 360-day calendar with twelve months of 30 days each. Although this was first seen in the Mesopotamian region, author and Egyptologist Geraldine Pinch describes how "certain stars and constellations had long been prominent in Egyptian religion, the twelve signs of the zodiac [. . .] appear on coffins in Roman Egypt, and the Graeco-Egyptian magical papyri include lists of the types of magic which could most successfully be worked under each star-sign." The biggest contrast with the Mesopotamian era was that classical Egyptian thinkers believed that the most accurate way to use astrology was to "understand the operation of divine will, not to predict or influence petty human affairs."

Egyptians used astrological placements and the calendar to monitor natural occurrences. For instance, the Nile river flooded every June, which irrigated the fields and prevented famine—crucial to the livelihood of Egyptian farmers. But if the flood was too strong, the waters could destroy crops and villages. Ancient Egyptian priests paid attention to the celestial bodies for each occurrence. They recorded the times of the rising of the Sun and of any important stars each day and noted which celestial events preluded a flood.

Egyptian priests recorded and kept track of multiple phenomena, and they assigned the name of a god to each season. The summer solstice, referred to as "The Birth of Re," the Sun god, made it easy for the average Egyptian to remember these calendrical occurrences. Leo Depuydt, professor of Egyptology and Assyriology, noted that as the civilizations merged during the first five millennia, it is possible that many Alexandrian scholars were Egyptian citizens of immigrant heritage—like astronomer Claudius Ptolemaeus (Ptolemy), who had a Latin-Macedonian name and wrote in Greek but lived in Egypt all of his life.

Ptolemy made astronomical and astrological observations and wrote on topics such as conjunctions, eclipses, transits, and occultations. His most well-known work is in a 13-book treatise called the *Almagest*, one of the most important works on astronomy and astrology, in which he details the motion and orbits of the Sun, Moon, and planets.

THE DECANS AND EGYPTIAN ASTROLOGY

The Egyptians were very focused on the "decans," a term that derives from the ancient Greek word *deka*, which means "ten." The decans are a minor rulership system, also called "faces" or *prosopon*. The decans divide each zodiac sign into three segments of ten degrees each, resulting in 36 decans in total. Each segment is ruled by a planet indicative of the triplicity or quadruplicity of the original domicile lord of the sign.

This practice places the planets in *heptazone* (the Chaldean order), meaning that they are placed in order of their motions: the Moon, Mercury, Venus, the Sun, Mars, Jupiter, and Saturn. The decans shaped the faces of the seven wandering stars (that we now know as planets) in relation to their decanic rulers. For instance, the sign Aries will be divided into three decans: 0 to 10 degrees of Aries or Mars, 10 to 20 degrees of Leo or the Sun, and 20 to 30 degrees of Sagittarius or Jupiter.

Ancient Egyptians created two types of star clocks, which also functioned as calendars, where one could read the hour of the night as well as the time of the year. The focus of Egyptian astrology was the movement of the stars associated with these decans, called the diurnal rotation, which would later be connected to the Mesopotamian twelve houses.

THE HELLENISTIC PERIOD

In the fourth century BCE, the Greeks colonized Babylonia and Egypt and came into contact with proto-astrology. A Babylonian priest named Berossus created a school of astrology for the Greeks on the island of Kos, where the study of Hippocratic medicine and the Asklepion healing sanctuary were located.

During the Hellenistic period—from 323 BCE to 31 BCE—Greek culture was at the forefront of philosophy, mathematics, astronomy, astrology, science, and the arts throughout the ancient world. Following the death of Alexander the Great, Greek culture expanded to the Persian and Arabic lands of the Ancient Near East.

ALEXANDRIA

According to American astrologer James Herschel Holden, Alexandria became an "important cultural and commercial center [...] where the cultural, religious, and scientific traditions of the ancient Greeks, Egyptians, and Babylonians were intermingled in one place." The Library of Alexandria was the largest library in the ancient world and contained thousands of texts from all around the globe. The city's cultural environment fostered intellectual, scientific, and artistic advancement. Naturally, Alexandria became a key place to study astrology and astronomy.

The idea of astral divination through omens spread from Babylonia to Egypt, where decans and star clocks were incorporated, and on to Greece. Hellenistic astrology combined many of the divination techniques from these earlier cultures to create what we know as modern astrology, featuring the house divisions, astrological signs, the lots, and the association of Greek myths to the planets.

THE ROMAN EMPIRE

The Roman Republic dominated the Mediterranean region for the first and second centuries BCE. In the first century BCE, the end of the Hellenistic period coincided with the expansion of the Roman Empire and the death of Julius Caesar.

During the funeral of Julius Caesar, a comet traveled through the sky and was seen as a sign from heaven, an omen that Caesar had acquired the status of a god (despite the fact that comets were normally seen as bad omens). His adopted son Augustus and the Roman Senate deified Caesar in accordance with this omen. Augustus took political advantage of the situation and murdered his father's assassins, Brutus and Cassius, and then commemorated Caesar with the building of the Temple of Mars Ultor in Rome. Augustus also began to use iconographic images on coins and statues of his adoptive father with a star above his head representing the comet.

Augustus connected himself to his father's godlike status to seem godlike as well. Though this was most likely a political move, it showed that, as celestial messages from the gods, astronomical and astrological occurrences of natural divination played a role in Roman society.

In the biography of Augustus by the historian Suetonius, Augustus went with his friend Agrippa to visit the astrologer and diviner Theogenes. Initially, Augustus was hesitant to have his natal chart read for fear that he would be determined unfit for his position, but this soon changed:

> "Being persuaded, however, after much importunity, to declare [his nativity], Theogenes started up from his seat and paid [Augustus] adoration. Not long afterwards, Augustus was so confident of the greatness of his destiny, that he published his horoscope, and struck a silver coin, bearing upon it the sign of Capricorn, under the influence of which he was born."

It's possible that because of this, individual natal horoscopes, or *themata*, became associated with individual power and claims to royalty or connections to the gods. At the Roman Empire's pinnacle of power, Hellenistic astrology—now practiced inside and outside of Greece—saw a huge resurgence until the seventh century CE.

AUGUSTUS AND THE CAPRICORN CLAIM TO POWER

Augustus was listed as a Libra Sun sign, but his Moon or rising sign was most likely Capricorn. Unlike today, where the Sun sign is seen as the most important determination of someone's personality, in Hellenistic astrology the Moon sign was viewed as a more accurate depiction of an individual's character. As Capricorn is connected with the planet Saturn and with power, authority, discipline, and sternness, it is no surprise that Augustus, the first emperor of Rome, would use this placement as a claim to natural power.

According to Roman mythology, the god Saturn, after falling from the heavens, created heaven on Earth in Italy, leading to a golden age of strength and virility for the country. In claiming his power on the throne, Augustus first linked himself to his deified father, Julius Caesar, and then to the god Saturn himself. Augustus restored Rome to glory by instituting social reforms and creating a focus on Roman art, literature, architecture, and religion, as well as conquering neighboring nations and winning multiple victories. After his rule of fifty-six years, he was also deified and considered a god.

DECLINE AND TRANSMISSION

By the third century CE, Rome was unable to sustain its expensive empire and began to decline in power and influence. After the rule of Augustus, Rome suffered under emperors who did not continue his strong Saturnian mindset and Venusian focus on fairness. These included Tiberius (14–37 CE), who was highly unpopular and cruel, and Marcus Aurelius (161–180 CE), who proposed war on Armenia and Parthia before his own empire was invaded by Germanic tribes from the north.

The imposition of other cultures, namely the Parthians and Germanic tribes, led to a change in political, cultural, intellectual, and religious ways of thinking and operating. Christianity, a monotheistic religion, gained in popularity. Roman emperor Constantine the Great legalized Christianity within the Roman Empire with the Edict of Milan in 313 CE. As Christianity opposes the fatalist view that the lives of individuals are predetermined to some degree by their birth charts, astrology and Christianity could not coexist.

Indeed, Saint John Chrysostom, archbishop of Constantinople, stated that "in truth, no doctrine is so depraved, bordering on incurable madness as the doctrine of fate and astrology." Successive emperors continued this negative view of astrology, including Eastern Roman emperor Justinian I, who declared astrology heresy. He ordered the burning of astrology books and exiled or banished astrologers from the city.

One of the biggest shifts in the Roman Empire was the movement of the capital city from Rome to Constantinople (modern-day Istanbul, Turkey). This created a separation of the empires, one to the west in Rome, which was on a steep decline, and one to the east in Constantinople, which flourished. In 476 CE, the Western Roman Empire was overtaken by Germanic Visigoths, when emperor Romulus Augustus, referred to by some scholars as the last Western Roman emperor, was overthrown.

Even though the Germanic invaders had their own connection to the stars in lunar months and lucky days, it was, as astrologer Nicholas Campion suggested, a far cry from "horoscopic astrology, with its literary base and mathematical complexities, [which] was not part of their culture." In 529 CE, the Eastern Roman Empire pushed the study of astrology underground, especially as philosophical schools were closed and there were bans across Athens on teaching "pagan" philosophy.

Astrology was pushed further and further away from the developing Christian Roman Empire. Elsewhere, though, the practices and techniques of astrology were translated and transmitted to other cultures and countries, including India, Persia, and the medieval Islamic Empire.

Greeks and Romans traded with India and settled there, bringing with them texts on Hellenistic astrology, which were later translated into Sanskrit. In 149 CE, this translated text, known as the *Yavanajataka*, or "Horoscopy of the Greeks," became the backbone of Indian astrology for the next two thousand years. Indians merged Hellenistic astrology with their own cosmologies and ideas, such as karma, Ayurveda, chakras, and Hindu deities, creating an amalgamized form of Hindu astrology.

As Brennan notes, Hindu astrology is probably more closely linked to ancient Hellenistic astrology than Western astrology is today, as Indian astrology has been essentially continuous since the second century CE. Western astrology, meanwhile, has been translated and retranslated numerous times, and each translation loses some of the subtle nuance of the original ideas.

In Persia, the works of Dorotheus of Sidon and Vettius Valens were translated into Pahlavi around the third century CE. The practice of Hellenistic astrology continued during the Sasanian Period in Persia. By the middle of the eighth century, the texts of Hellenistic astrology had entered the Islamic Empire. The Abbasid rulers collected a group of astrologers to use electional or inceptional astrology to determine an auspicious location for the capital of their empire, and as a result, it was moved from Damascus to Baghdad.

REDISCOVERY AND REVIVAL

Whereas astrology flourished in the Asian and Arabic regions between the seventh and tenth centuries, the Western world had forgotten the lore and understanding of Hellenistic astrology. It was denigrated as being "evil" and forbidden by the Catholic Church.

In the Byzantine Empire, many of the Hellenistic works, along with the works of Arabic astrologers, all now translated into Persian and Arabic, survived and began to make their way around the world. Byzantine emperor Manuel I (1143–1180 CE) used astrology to determine his political affairs, similar to the original use of Hellenistic astrology in Mesopotamia. Many of these texts then made their way to Europe, particularly to Moorish libraries in southern Spain. These were translated into Latin by scholars like Robert of Chester, Abraham Ibn Ezra, Plato of Tivoli, and Hermann of Carinthia.

During the 13th and 14th centuries, the translated Latin texts made their way to medieval universities and were taught as a science validated by the Aristotelian cosmology of medical astrology. Rulers again began to use royal astrologers or chart-casters to guide them in political and social decisions. With the fall of Constantinople in 1453, the triumphant Turks brought a host of Greek and Latin texts and scholars to Italy. This started the rebirth of classical humanism, paganism, and mysticism that characterizes the Italian Renaissance, which lasted from the 14th to the 17th centuries.

During the Renaissance, astrology became popular again, with practitioners and astrologers refining and testing many of the calculations and practices used in previous texts. The focus on divination and magic came to the forefront, casting doubt on the possibility of free will. This angered the Catholic and Protestant churches, which continued to condemn the practice of astrology.

By the 18th century, during the Age of Reason and the Enlightenment, in accordance with works like Copernicus's heliocentric model of the Universe, scholars attempted to debunk the validity of astrology. The practice of astrology fell into ill repute, as it was not connected to scientific thought, and it went underground again.

In Britain, the Spiritualism movement of the 19th century allowed people to explore astrology in addition to occult practices, such as those involving the supernatural and ghosts. The Theosophical movement brought to the West the Eastern ideas of karma and reincarnation. Over 50 years, Belgian historian Franz Cumont and German philologist Franz Boll translated into English many of the scattered astrological texts from all around the world. This resulted in the 12-volume *Catalog of Greek Astrological Codices*. These new ideas became tools for self-realization, as they connected depth psychology, spirituality, the supernatural, and other dimensions that related to the underlying notions of astrology. The birth chart was again seen as a tool to understand the psyche and soul evolution within the cosmos. Today, astrological scholars have worked tirelessly to translate many of the Greek, Latin, Arabic, and Persian texts.

Hellenistic astrology rode the wave from academic acclaim to the depths of being pushed underground by religious doctrine. The core tenets have survived, however, having made their way into modern astrology, and we will study these in greater depth in the following chapter.

CHAPTER 2

The Seven Wandering Stars

Ancient Hellenistic astrologers envisioned the sky and the cosmos as an interconnecting web of planetary structures with the Earth at the center. The surrounding celestial bodies, with their unpredictable and irregular movements, were called "the seven wandering stars." The seven consisted of five planets—Saturn (Kronos), Jupiter (Zeus), Mars (Ares), Venus (Aphrodite), and Mercury (Hermes)—and two luminaries, the Moon (Selene) and the Sun (Helios). Ancient Babylonian and Greek astrologers gave the planets names connected to their gods. For example, the Babylonians referred to the Sun as Shamash, the god of justice and divination, whereas the Greeks called it Helios, the god who sees all.

Each planet, from a cosmological perspective, is said to embody the nature, characteristics, and energy of the gods associated with it. The energy of the planet is then transmitted through the divine realm to mortals on Earth, who, according to the hierarchy of the cosmos, are in the center of this divine orchestration. Following the principle "as above, so below," a Mercurial person will embody the energies of the god Hermes: quick-witted, intelligent, and prone to boredom. Now we will consider the original meanings of these luminaries as they fit into the hierarchy of the cosmos.

SPHERE OF THE FIXED STARS
SPHERE OF SATURN
SPHERE OF JUPITER
SPHERE OF MARS
SPHERE OF THE SUN
SPHERE OF VENUS
SPHERE OF MERCURY
SPHERE OF THE MOON

EARTH

The Sun (Helios)

According to Greek mythology, Helios, the god of the Sun, was said to ride his golden chariot across the sky every day, carrying the Sun from the East to the West. He is the bringer of "fiery, intelligent light." The energy of Helios is strong and determined. It rules the right eye, heart, spine, and upper back.

Sun energy represents the soul as a part of our mind that is essential to our existence. The Sun has heating, drying, and bitter qualities, so an overabundance of this quality can "dry out" those around you or result in too much energy expended on a particular idea, person, or event. It rules the paternal or father energy and can represent rulers, public reputation and engagement, and the qualities of nobility, action, leadership, authority, and judgment, as well as statues and crowns. The Sun is represented by the color yellow and by the crops wheat and barley.

Astrologically, the Sun is associated with the sign Leo. Among Babylonian, Greek, and Roman gods, the Sun is associated with Shamash, Helios, and Apollo, respectively, all of whom were represented with beams of light emanating from their heads. They are the bringers of light and knowledge, meant to illuminate others with their life force. Leos and the Sun are the bringers of joy, happiness, and strength in all situations. Sun people may be seen leading groups, promoting ideas, and aiding those in need, like a father figure. They are part of the diurnal (daytime) sect.

The Moon (Selene)

The Moon is associated with the gods Luna (Roman), Selene (Greek), and Sin (Babylonian). The Moon is connected with the physical self, the nocturnal, travel, femininity, receptivity, lawful marriages or cohabitation, housekeeping, the older sibling, the queen, the mistress of the house, possessions, and fortune. The Moon exudes a humidifying and slightly warming quality. It rules the left eye, the stomach, the breasts, the spleen, and the marrow and is associated with silver, glass, Monday, and the color green. It is salty in taste.

The strongest connection to the Moon is that of the mother, our nurturing nature, or of conception, as the nature of the Moon is to nourish, provide foresight, and act as a caretaker. The Sun and Moon are the ruling luminaries in one's life—the Sun is seen as king, the right eye, and the father, whereas the Moon is seen as the queen, the left eye, and the mother. They both exhibit the key aspects of our personalities, whereas the other planets act as ministers or servants to assist in actualizing these forces in our lives.

Saturn (Kronos)

Saturn was called Kronos (Greek), associated with old age and death, Saturnus (Roman), the god of agriculture, and Ninurta (Babylon), the god of sickness, war, death, irrigation, and agriculture. The themes of the planet Saturn are sources of long-lasting punishment, misery, disrepute, slander, deceit, sullenness, the elderly, elder brothers, captivity, exposure, and tears.

Saturn has a destructive life force in nature because it is excessively cold and moderately dry. It is constrictive, castor-like in color, and astringent in taste. Saturn is associated with lead, wood, and stone and is connected to Saturday. The Saturnine person is predisposed to silence, depression, anxiety, sorrow, grief, lack of emotional display, and inaction. Due to the cold nature of Saturn, it can represent long-lasting complaints from the cold temperature.

The body parts associated with Saturn are the thighs, knees, lymph nodes, bladder, and kidneys, as well as the conditions of gout and hidden injuries. Saturn can lead someone to become an administrator, manager, farmer, laborer, tax collector, or landlord and provide an abundance in money, property, family, inheritance, and power.

Although Kronos can represent fear and power struggles, it can also indicate the tendency to persevere. The nature of Saturn and Saturnine people is to power through adversity, to build and create and then to manifest a legacy.

SATURN (KRONOS) DEVOURING HIS SON

In Greek mythology, Ouranos, also called Uranus, emerged from Gaea or Gaia, representative of the Earth, who came into existence from Chaos, where all things were said to begin. The two of them gave birth to seven children, represented by the seven wandering stars, who were later called the seven Titans.

Saturn or Kronos, who became leader of the Titans, feared his children overtaking him and ruling the kingdom, so he began to eat them as they were born. His partner Rhea managed to save one child, Zeus, and hid him away on Crete. When Zeus grew up, he forced Kronos to disgorge his siblings. Zeus then killed Kronos and became the leader of Mount Olympus. This myth is portrayed in the famous painting by Francisco Goya *Saturn Devouring His Son* (c. 1819–1823).

Jupiter (Zeus)

The ancient Babylonians knew Jupiter as Marduk; to the ancient Greeks it was Zeus. Both gods battle dragons to establish order in the cosmos and become the supreme leader of the gods. As such, Jupiter represents the protector of the state and the guardian of law, justice, and fate. A Jupiterian person can be a good, wise leader, rich in friendships, with abundance, intelligence, and a religious connection. They are free-spirited, open-minded, and often the recipient of widespread honors, awards, and acclaim.

Jupiter represents the warm, moist energy that creates a productive life force within. It is the main determinant of childbearing and children. It rules over the thighs, feet, liver, sperm, uterus, and also the masculine, right side of the body. It is light gray, sweet in taste, and connected to Thursday and tin.

A Jupiterian person can be someone who is egotistical and high-minded and begrudges progress in life. However, the overriding nature of Jupiter is to expand and affirm. Much like Zeus, who was said to know all, it is meant for Jupiter to know more and to become knowledgeable. Jupiter can be connected to the archetype of the Sage, the Priest, and the Great Man.

Mars (Ares)

The ancient Babylonians knew Mars as Nergal, the god of the underworld, fevers, plagues, and war. Similarly, the ancient Greeks associated him with Ares, the god of war, violence, and anger. Mars is the destructive life force that appears in human nature. Mars is fiery, hot, and dry, and it rules the head, the buttocks, the back, bile, and excretion. It is associated with iron, wine, beans, and the color red. It can be pungent in taste. This planet can be connected with sexual impulses, adulteries, abortion, and the "procreative impulse."

The Romans perceived a more toned-down version of the planet with the connection to Martus, the protector of empires through military prowess and valor. A Martian person can embody the qualities of recklessness, violence, danger, the hunt and the chase, lawsuits, and theft.

There are also positive aspects of this planet: courage, valor, strength, leadership, a warrior's spirit, daring, and conscious masculinity. As the planet Mars is associated with the god of war, it is connected with the archetypes of the Warrior and the Competitor. It is meant to energize the individual for productive motivations.

Venus (Aphrodite)

The ancient Babylonians envisioned Venus as Ishtar, the goddess of love, fertility, and land. Similarly, the ancient Greeks dubbed her Aphrodite, goddess of beauty and desire. Venus is moist and warming, allowing for productivity to occur. She signifies worship, love, beauty, cleanliness, laughter, joy, play, aquatic animals, and the ability to receive. She is also associated with femininity, purity, religious worship, and all women—the mother, sister, daughter, grandmother, and aunt. She rules over marriage and the benefits of civilization. Her nature is cheerful and optimistic, drenched in adornments and gold, and she is skilled in the arts—singing, dancing, acting, playing an instrument, sewing, embroidery, dyeing fabric, and working with crystals or precious stones.

Venus rules the face, the neck, the sense of smell, the front of the body, the lungs, and the genitals. The planet is also associated with precious stones and the color white, and it can be oily in taste. Venus can exhibit jealousy, hate, and envy, but the core essence of Venus is to love, desire, and adore and to receive those emotions in return. As Venus is associated with the goddesses of love and friendship, it can be associated with the archetypes of the Lover and the Harmonizer or Mediator.

Mercury (Hermes)

The ancient Greeks connected Mercury to the god Hermes, the winged messenger of Zeus who delivered messages to the gods. He was the patron of writing, the sciences, travel, athletics, luck, and commerce. He was also the protector of thieves and a psychopomp—a guide to the underworld.

Mercury exhibits qualities that are quick and ever changing and can be wet or dry. This planet is connected with language, intelligence, brotherhood, interpretation, writing, calculations, commerce, youth, play, theft, community, marketing, banking, friendship, knowledge, and forethought. Mercurial people make great orators, astrologers, philosophers, scribes, prophets, augurs, dream interpreters, musicians, and architects.

Mercury can also indicate youth and working with your hands. Mercury rules the hands, fingers, shoulders, intestines, tongue, and hearing and corresponds to the color blue, to a sharp taste, and to copper or brass. A person can utilize the positive aspects of this planet by becoming industrious, of sound judgment, sociable, ingenious, and respectable. Conversely, Mercury can lead to madness, ecstasy, melancholy, and capriciousness. Mercury is associated with the archetype of the Messenger.

Distinctions, Characteristics, and Qualities

In this section, we will discuss additional distinctions, character-istics, and qualities of the planets. These features are important to determine, as they shift the definition of the planetary energy in accordance to the rest of the birth chart. This section will cover the definitions of all of these attributes, the morning and evening star, as well as the speed, retrograde, and stations of a planet.

BENEFIC AND MALEFIC

Hellenistic astrology explores both the "good" and "evil" attributes of each planet, which is necessary in determining one's birth chart. In astrology, the "good" attributes are called "benefic," a term that means "good-maker" and is derived from the ancient Greek word *agathopoios*. "Malefic" is a term that means "bad-maker" and is derived from the Greek word *kakopoios*.

Astrologers and philosophers alike understand that good and evil coexist. The Greek Stoic philosopher Chrysippus made a strong case for good and evil existing simultaneously within the same energy: one cannot exist without the other. Removing one, you remove both. Nothing is wholly positive, and nothing is wholly negative.

Venus and Jupiter are seen as benefic planets. Their general nature and disposition bring about positive outcomes in the life of the individual, such as prosperity, happiness, and success. Mars and Saturn are viewed as malefic planets. Their general nature and disposition bring about problems in the life of the individual, such as poverty, bankruptcy, failure, or suffering. Mercury, the Sun, and the Moon are viewed as "common" or neutral. They have the capacity to operate in a benefic or malefic way, depending on the planet in conjunction with them.

Benefic and malefic energies can be seen in the classification of the gods associated with each planet. For instance, Jupiter is associated with Zeus, the god of prosperity, abundance, and knowledge, which are all positive energies.

Remember that the planets themselves are not inherently good or bad. The Hellenistic astrologer Plotinus argues that "there are no bad planets because they are divine, and they do not contain a cause of evil in their nature." An abundance of Jupiter is meant to bestow the individual with good luck, stamina, confidence, and healthy competition. In excess, though, this energy can foster malicious competition, arrogance, overeagerness, and the feeling that one is invincible to life's foibles.

SECTS

A sect, referred to as *hairesis* in ancient Greek, means an alliance, faction, or identification with a school of thought, a party, or a team. There are two forms of sects: day (or diurnal), with the Sun as the ruler, and night (or nocturnal), with the Moon as the ruler.

The Sun and the Moon, the two great luminaries, or "sect lights," are the leaders of the sects that light the way for the other planets. The Sun and the Moon reflect each other. The Sun represents direct thought and the mind, whereas the Moon represents the body, emotions, and feelings. Determining the sect shows which luminary dominates the essence of an individual's life and destiny. Each sect team has one benefic, one malefic, and one neutral planet. The Sun holds Jupiter, Saturn, and Mercury on the diurnal sect team, whereas the Moon holds Venus, Mars, and Mercury on the nocturnal sect team. Due to Mercury's duplicity, it is capable of joining either team depending on the time of day (which further enforces Mercury's reputation of duality and changeability).

BIRTH TIME AND THE ASCENDANT

If you do not have the birth time of an individual to determine if the chart is diurnal or nocturnal, or if the time of day is not clear, you can determine the sect of a birth chart by looking at the degrees of the Ascendant and Descendant. In a whole house sign chart, this will be in the first and seventh houses, respectively.

You are looking for the place where the sky meets the Earth on the horizon. If the Sun lies above the horizon, then the person has a daytime, or diurnal, sect chart, and they were born during the day. If the Sun lies below the horizon, then the person was born at night and possesses a nighttime, or nocturnal, sect chart.

MASCULINE AND FEMININE

The masculine and feminine qualities of the planets play an interesting role in planet classification. Mercury is common or neutral, but leans more toward the masculine energy than the feminine. Venus and the Moon are considered feminine energies that represent a cooling or slowing down of energies, being receptive and open to engagement.

The Sun, Saturn, Mars, Jupiter, and Mercury are considered to be masculine energies, prone to act and respond in a faster way and be more open to change. This can make events involving the masculine planets happen sooner.

MORNING STAR, EVENING STAR

Another consideration is determining which planets are the morning stars (*heoia*) and which are the evening stars (*hesperia*). The former rises over the horizon before the Sun on the native's (the person associated with a given birth chart) day of birth, while the latter sets under the horizon on the native's day of birth. Originally, the terms "morning star" and "evening star" were applied only to the two brightest stars and innermost planets, Venus and Mercury.

The French astronomer Camille Flammarion called Venus "The Shepherd's Star," referring to its consistent brightness as the star that led the Magi to the infant Jesus. The planet Mercury, also a bright star, had different names according to the time of day. It was referred to as Apollo in the morning and Mercury in the evening. Similarly, Venus was Phosphorus in the morning and Hesperus in the evening. According to Ptolemy and Porphyry, Mercury "joins the diurnal sect when he is a morning star, by rising before the Sun on the day of the native's birth, while he joins the nocturnal sect when he is an evening star, by setting after the Sun on the day of the native's birth."

Morning stars were seen as more masculine, active, and productive earlier in life because they rose before the Sun, whereas evening stars are said to be more feminine, passive, and inclined to produce things later in life.

SPEED, RETROGRADE, AND STATIONS

A planet's speed, retrograde, and stations determine how quickly the qualities of the planet can connect with an individual. Stations refer to planetary transits as viewed from Earth, which change in motion from direct (or forward) and retrograde (or backward). Valens notes that retrograde planets "delay expectations, actions, profits, and enterprises," while when a planet station is direct, it "removes any hindrances and restores and leads to the stability and rectification of life."

Over the course of 24 hours, a planet can move faster or slower than its ordinary rate of speed. Faster movement is called "addictive" (*prosthetikos*), which signals that the planetary energy and sign will manifest faster or sooner in the native's life. A slowing down of the planet is called "subtractive" (*aphairetikos*), which means the energy will manifest at a slower rate or at a later time for the native.

Chapter 1 gave us an overview of the development of Hellenistic astrology, and in this chapter, we discussed the ideologies, myths, and qualities associated with the planets. In the next chapter, we will explore the energies of the zodiac signs.

CHAPTER 3

The Signs of the Zodiac

The planets are important: They represent the physical, mental, emotional, and spiritual manifestations that pervade our human existence. They help us recognize our destiny, life purpose, and focus by reflecting the energy and characteristics of the gods within our personalities.

In this chapter, we will explore the twelve astrological signs derived from these planets. We will also look at a number of other aspects that can be used to explore the relationship between planets and signs, such as planetary rulership, domicile rulership, gender, exaltations and depressions, triplicities, and quadruplicities.

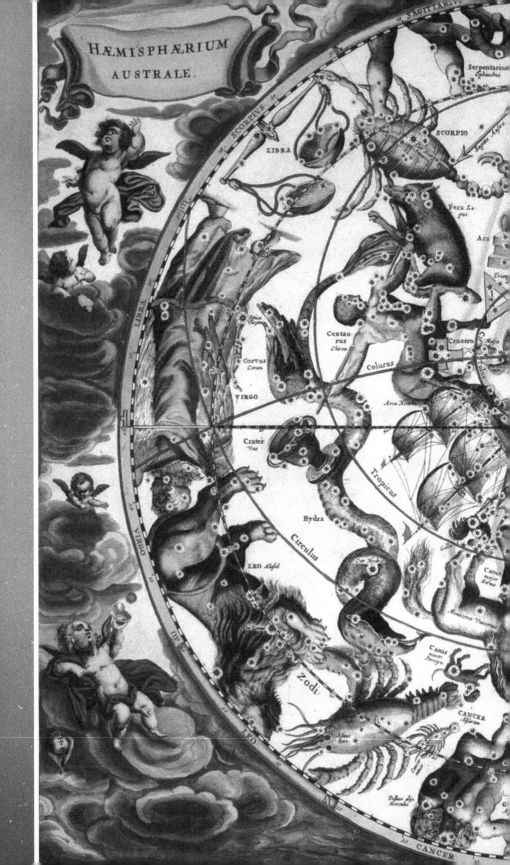

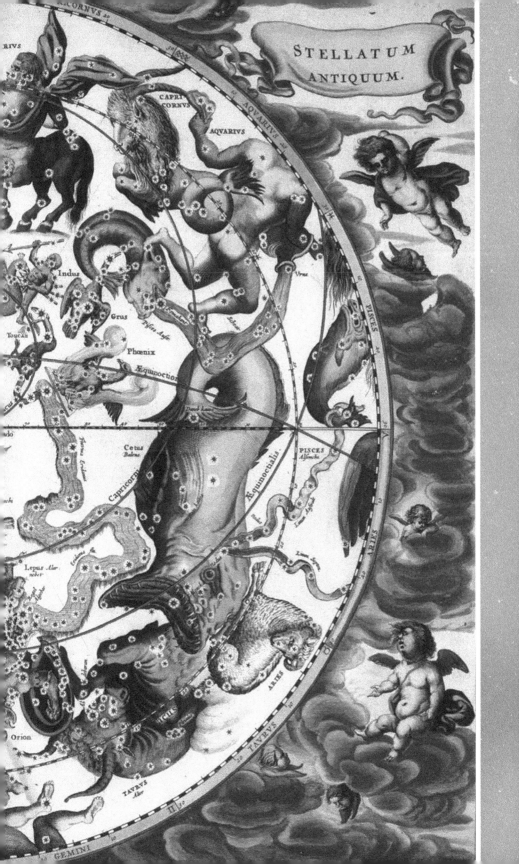

STELLATUM
ANTIQUUM.

Understanding the Ecliptic

Ancient astrologers and astronomers tracked the movement of the original seven wandering stars, constellations, and fixed stars as they moved across the sky. These academics believed that the Earth was the focal point of the Universe. Referring to the Thema Mundi, or the Nativity of the Cosmos, a mythical horoscope that depicts the position of the planets at the beginning of the Universe (page 48), Hellenistic astrologers determined that the narrow, circular path that guided the planets' journey through the night sky around the Earth was called the ecliptic.

Between the fifth and seventh centuries BCE, Mesopotamians divided the ecliptic circle into 12 equal parts of 30 degrees each, equaling 360 degrees in total. The Babylonians ascertained the same 360 days by watching the Sun's yearly ecliptic path around the Earth. The Egyptians used this theory of degrees in the ecliptic path and connected it with the number of degrees in a circle, also echoing the circular ecliptic path of the Sun around the Earth.

The word "zodiac" derives from the ancient Greek term *zoidiakos kyklos*, which means "cycle [or circle] of little animals." The images of living beings in the corresponding constellations became connected to the twelve signs of the zodiac. The zodiac connected innate characteristics of these beings to particular signs.

Tropical Zodiac and Sidereal Zodiac

By the fifth century BCE in Mesopotamia, the term "zodiac" referenced the twelve astrological signs within the ecliptic circle. This created two types of zodiac: sidereal and tropical. Both zodiacs offer insight into the character, attributes, and destiny of the sign, planet, or individual. Both types divide the zodiac into 12 signs of 30 degrees each.

The sidereal zodiac derives from the Latin *sidereus*, meaning "star" or "constellation," and explores our relationship with the fixed stars and constellations. The sidereal zodiac is determined by the size of the constellations. For instance, Taurus is a large constellation that overflows into the neighboring star cluster, the Pleiades. In the sidereal zodiac, the calculations for all zodiac signs are seen as equal, even though the size of the constellation is not. Therefore, the sidereal zodiac can be seen as a symbolic representation of the twelve zodiac signs even though it does not align with the actual signs themselves.

The tropical zodiac, on the other hand, which is what most Western astrologers use today, coincides with the four seasons and begins and ends at the exact degree of the two solstices and two equinoxes—the points in the year when the Sun travels north and south of the equator. The starting point of the year in the tropical zodiac begins with Aries, or the spring equinox. The rest of the seasons correlate with the beginning points of each of the other cardinal signs: Cancer, Libra, and Capricorn. The middle of the seasons coincides with the fixed signs: Taurus, Leo, Scorpio, and Aquarius. Lastly, the seasons end with the mutable signs: Gemini, Virgo, Sagittarius, and Pisces.

ANIMALS AND THE ZODIAC

The attributes of the animal or being are mirrored in the attributes of its zodiac sign. For example, Aries the Ram can be aggressive and forceful, and one would not want to confront an angry ram (or Aries). In contrast, Aquarius the Water Bearer can be peaceful and giving to others. The image of someone pouring water is synonymous with the idea that Aquarius gives their "water," or life force, to others while taking none for themself. Those born under Libra the Scales will have a deep-seated need to constantly "balance the scales" and may have a difficult time determining their own needs and opinions while trying to keep others happy.

Delineating the Signs

Regardless of the type of zodiac, the twelve astrological signs were connected to and named for the constellations that they either were a part of or encompassed wholly in the night sky. Each constellation was associated with the person, animal, or object that represented the sign, such as Aries the Ram, Gemini the Twins, Virgo the Virgin, Libra the Scales, Sagittarius the Archer, and Aquarius the Water-bearer. The names of the twelve astrological signs derive from the traditional Greek constellations compiled by Ptolemy in the second century BCE.

ARIES (KRIOS)

Aries, referred to as Krios by the ancient Greeks, is identified with the story of the ram that saved Phrixus. Phrixus and his twin sister Helle were the children of Athamus, a Boeotian king. Their step-mother was jealous of the children and wanted them dead. She concocted a duplicitous plan with the Oracle at Delphi to have the children sacrificed in order to rejuvenate dying crops and end the ongoing famine. As the two children were about to die, their real mother, a cloud nymph named Nephele, sent a winged ram with golden wool to rescue them. The Golden Ram, named Chrysomallus, was originally the human daughter of Poseidon and Theophane before the gods turned her into a ram with magical abilities.

The Golden Ram flew to Colchis with the children, but only Phrixus survived. He was greeted by Aeëtes, the king of Colchis, who allowed Phrixus to marry his daughter Chalciope in exchange for the ram's golden fleece. This same golden fleece would be seen as a sought-after prize in other Greek myths, including that of Jason and the Argonauts.

The ancient Babylonians believed the constellation of Aries to be the final journey on the ecliptic or diurnal rotation. In 130 BCE, the Greeks determined that because Aries was so close to the spring equinox and spring was equated with the beginning of life, it was proper for Aries to be the first astrological sign on the diurnal rotation instead.

TAURUS (TAUROS)

Taurus is one of the oldest constellations in the sky. The constellation of Taurus is made up of multiple stars, with Aldebaran (or Alpha Tauri) being the brightest. The best way to locate Taurus is to find the constellation Orion and then look northeast for the bright, orange star of Aldebaran, named for the Arabic word *al Dabarān*, which means "the follower." This star is also known as the "angry eye of Taurus the Bull." Taurus and its nearest star cluster, the Pleiades, were known as the Bull and the Seven Sisters, respectively.

The Greek myth behind Taurus tells of Zeus and Europa, the beautiful daughter of Agenor, the Phoenician king. Zeus fell in love with Europa and disguised himself as a handsome bull to get her attention. They had many children together. To commemorate their love, prosperity, and the birth of their three sons, Zeus placed Taurus, a constellation resembling the horns of the bull, in the sky.

Taurus marks the middle of spring. The qualities of Taurus are exemplified in the story of Zeus and Europa as well as in the story of the Cretan Bull, representing love, loyalty, wealth, prosperity, a hardworking nature, builders, and property as well as stubbornness, aggression, violence, and power.

GEMINI (DIDUMOI)

Gemini (or Didumoi) is the 30th-largest constellation in the sky in the second quadrant of the Northern Hemisphere. It's personified by "the Twins," or "the Dioscuri," Castor and Pollux.

The symbol of Gemini is connected to the duplicity of the twins, Castor and Pollux, who were the sons of Zeus and the Spartan queen Leda. The two brothers were inseparable. When Castor was killed during a fight with Idas and Lynceus of Messenia, Pollux gave up his immortality to be transformed by Zeus into the constellation Gemini. In the parts of the cosmos represented by the Thema Mundi,

Gemini is seen to represent the twelfth place of the cosmos, as Cancer was seen to be the Ascendant of the Earth.

The Twins were the patron saints of shipwrecked sailors, due to Gemini's connection to travel and movement, as well as siblings and education. Gemini is characterized by a fondness for discourse and education, as well as being critics of good and bad, being initiated in cult matters, and being poetic.

CANCER (KARKINOS)

Cancer (or Karkinos) the Crab lies in the second quadrant of the Northern Hemisphere near Canis Minor, Gemini, Hydra, Leo, Leo Minor, and Lynx. The Beehive Cluster (of which the brightest stars are Al Tarf and Beta Cancri) are found in the Cancer constellation.

In Greek mythology, the sign of Cancer is connected to the Twelve Labors of Heracles (the Greek name for Hercules). As Heracles was fighting the Lernaean Hydra, the serpentine multiheaded beast, his sworn enemy, the goddess Hera, sent a large crab, called the Carcinus, to distract him during the fight. In one ending of this myth, Heracles kicked the crab into the sky. In another, he crushed the crab, and Hera placed a constellation in the sky to commemorate it.

Cancer is associated with the Ascendant of the cosmos, as well as the breasts and the ribs. In modern astrology, it is associated with the devotion that the crab exhibited toward its "mother" Hera. Therefore, the personality traits associated with Cancer are a loving disposition, strong emotion, and the inability to go straight toward what it wants, just as a crab moves from side to side and doesn't confront things directly.

LEO (LEON)

Leo (or Leon) the Lion is one of the largest constellations in the second quadrant of the Northern Hemisphere and the twelfth-largest in the entire night sky. The brightest stars in the Leo constellation form the Sickle of Leo, a distinguishing feature that is easy to spot. The brightest star, Regulus (or Alpha Leonis), marks the lion's heart.

Algieba (or Gamma Leonis) marks the lion's neck, and Adhafera (or Zeta Leonis), Rasalas (or Mu Leonis), and Algenubi (or Epsilon Leonis) make up the lion's mane and head. Leo is one of the oldest constellations in the sky.

The ancient Greeks associated Leo with the Nemean lion, the animal Heracles killed as one of his Twelve Labors in penance for killing his family. This lion lived in a cave, had impenetrable skin, and would often kill locals. Heracles could not kill the lion head-on, so he trapped it in a cave and strangled it to death. He continued to wear a cloak made of the lion's impenetrable fur both for his own personal protection and in admiration of the lion—as well as to intimidate his enemies. Heracles, the strongest warrior, was so impressed with the Nemean lion that he placed it in the sky for its ability to challenge him, making it the king of beasts.

This story exemplifies the energy and qualities of the lion: strength, determination, and perseverance. Leo is ruled by the Sun and is viewed as the king of the zodiac. Personality traits include unflappability, being well-tempered, intellectual, just, and also possibly tyrannical or kingly. Showing strength along with the mental ability to best your opponents is exemplified by the myth of Heracles and the Nemean lion.

VIRGO (PARTHENOS)

Virgo (or Parthenos) the Virgin is the largest constellation of the zodiac and the second-largest constellation in the night sky. Virgo appears in the Northern Hemisphere during the autumnal equinox alongside Leo, Libra, Serpens Caput, Bootes, Coma Berenices, Corvus, and Crater.

Virgo, which is Latin for "virgin," is personified as an actual virgin with angelic wings and an ear of wheat in her left hand, which is represented by the bright star Spica. The constellation of Virgo is associated with the Greek goddess of justice, Dike, the daughter of Zeus and the Titaness Themis, who gave a speech urging humans to continue to honor the gods during the Iron Age. When humans began warring with one another and living inharmoniously, she turned her back to them and flew to the heavens, placing herself in the sky.

This constellation is also connected to Persephone, the daughter of Demeter, the Greek goddess of the harvest. Persephone was abducted by Hades, the god of the underworld, an act that ended eternal spring on Earth. Located next to the constellation Libra and the scales of justice, Virgo is also interested in keeping things fair and just.

The fastidious and duty-bound qualities of the sign of Virgo can be seen in both stories. Dike defended her father, demanding that humans follow suit and continue to be duty-bound to the gods by worshipping them. Similarly, industriousness and other hardworking, mystical, and domestic attributes are connected to Demeter, the harvest goddess.

LIBRA (ZUGOS)

In the Southern Hemisphere, we find the constellation Libra (or Zugos), whose name is Latin for "weighing scales." As its name implies, it represents harmony and the balanced seasons. The symbol for Libra, the scales, is the only non-anthropomorphic representation of an astrological sign in the zodiac.

The scales of Libra are held by the Greek goddess of justice, Dike (from the constellation Virgo), and are associated with fate and fortune. With one scale representing fate and the other fortune, they are constantly balanced within the life of an individual. Libra is also associated with the Claws of Scorpio. Ancient Babylonians and Greeks associated Libra more with the Virgo qualities of justice and added the theme of balance to its representational characteristics.

The four brightest stars in the constellation form a quadrangle comprised of Alpha and Beta Librae, which depict the scales' balance beam, and Gamma and Sigma Librae, the scales' weighing pans. Libra is also home to the oldest star in the sky, Methuselah.

SCORPIO (SKORPIOS)

Also in the Southern Hemisphere, positioned near the center of the Milky Way and next to Libra and Sagittarius, Scorpius (which lends its name to the astrological sign Scorpio), or Skorpios, is one of the oldest constellations. Skorpios, translated from ancient Greek, means "creature with the burning sting" and was said to be the child of Gaia. A part of the Libra constellation, the "claw" of Scorpius is represented by the two brightest stars, Beta Librae and Alpha Librae (or Zubeneschamali and Zubenelgenubi, Arabic terms for "northern claw" and "southern claw," respectively). Scorpius also contains the bright stars Antares and Shaula and includes the Butterfly Cluster, the Cat Paw's Nebula, the Ptolemy Cluster, and the War and Peace Nebula.

There are two main myths associated with Scorpius. In one, Orion boasted that he was the best hunter and could kill every animal on Earth. Artemis and her mother, Leto, sent a scorpion to kill Orion, and after the battle, Zeus put the animal in the sky as a commemoration. In the other story, Artemis's twin brother, Apollo, was annoyed with Orion's boastfulness, as Orion had declared himself a better hunter than Artemis, and sent a scorpion to kill Orion.

Zeus placed both the scorpion and Orion in the sky, and both are visible in the sky at different points of the year. Scorpio is meant to exhibit treachery, theft, secret plotters, cunning, and unwavering loyalty.

SAGITTARIUS (TOXOTES)

In the center of the Milky Way is one of the largest constellations in the fourth quadrant of the Southern Hemisphere, Sagittarius (or Toxotes). Sagittarius represents the Archer, half-man and half-beast, holding a bow and arrow ready to shoot, aimed at the heart of neighboring Scorpius.

This constellation is associated with the satyr Crotus, a two-legged mythical creature with the body of a beast and the torso of a human, who nursed and cared for the Muses, daughters of Zeus, on Mount Helicon. Due to his diligent care of the Muses, they asked their father to place him in the sky.

In other mythologies, Sagittarius is represented as a centaur—a half-horse, half-human creature with the torso of a man and the legs and lower body of a horse. This centaur was said to have been sent by Orion to kill the scorpion who was sent to kill him. Many believe that the symbol of Sagittarius should be connected to the satyr rather than the centaur, as Crotus was the son of Pan and was said to have invented archery while living on Mount Helicon with the Muses.

The qualities of Sagittarius are those of a good-natured person, including a great soul, generosity, a fondness of brothers and friends, and a display of authority and versatility.

CAPRICORN (AIGOKEROS)

The constellation Capricornus (which lends its name to the astrological sign Capricorn) can be found in the Southern Hemisphere. Known in Greek as Aigokeros, which means "goat-horned," Capricornus is referred to as the sea goat, a creature that is half goat and half fish. Capricornus marks the winter solstice, beginning the astrological sign of Capricorn on the first day of winter.

Capricorn is associated with Pan, who had the legs and horns of a goat, with his son Crotus next to him as Sagittarius. Pan was commemorated by Zeus for rescuing the gods during times of war. While warring with the Titans, Pan blew his conch, scaring the Titans and warning Zeus that a monster, Typhon, sent by Gaia, was nearby. He also used his intellect to determine that the gods must disguise themselves as animals until Typhon passed. Pan went into the river and turned the lower part of his body into a fish to confuse the monster.

This depiction of a creature that is half goat and half fish is still synonymous with Capricorn. In another story, Capricorn is represented by the goddess, Amalthea, who protected and suckled Zeus as an infant when his father Cronus was devouring all of his children.

By protecting Zeus, she allowed him to survive and later fulfill the prophecy of overthrowing his father and rescuing his siblings from Cronus's stomach.

The qualities of Capricorn are exemplified in both stories: a strong sense of duty and loyalty, resourcefulness, intelligence, and being hardworking, as well as skill in deception, as both Pan and Amalthea deceived those who tried to hurt the ones they cared about.

AQUARIUS (HYDROCHOOS)

Aquarius (or Hydrochoos), which means "water-bearer" or "cup-bearer" in Latin, is one of the oldest constellations in the night sky. It can be seen in the spring in the Southern Hemisphere and in the fall in the Northern Hemisphere. Ancient Sumerians viewed Aquarius as Enki, the god of water.

Aquarius does not have bright stars and can be difficult to see with the naked eye. Aquarius is surrounded by other water-based constellations, including Cetus the Whale, Delphinus the Dolphin, Pisces the Fish, and Eridanus the River, in an area of the night sky called the Water or the Sea.

It is said that the symbolic, personified representation of Aquarius is through Ganymede, the son of the Trojan King Tros. Ganymede was a good-looking young man who was brought to Mount Olympus by Zeus, who disguised himself as an eagle (represented by the constellation Aquila, which is near Aquarius). Ganymede's role was to serve the gods and become their cupbearer, serving water, nectar, and ambrosia. Aquarius is a happy-go-lucky sign representing brotherhood, serving humanity, selflessness, connections to water, and friendliness.

PISCES (ICHTHUS)

Pisces (or Ichthus), which means "the fish" in Latin, represents the 14th-largest constellation overall, with very faint stars, similar to Cancer and Capricornus. The anthropomorphic representation of

Pisces is of two fish, one swimming north and the other swimming west, attached to each other by a cord. The end of this rope is the star Alrescha (or Alpha Piscium), which means "the cord" in Arabic. The constellation of Pisces lies between the Aries and Aquarius constellations and holds the point where the Sun crosses the celestial equator, marking the spring equinox in March.

In Roman mythology, the two fish that represent Pisces are manifestations of Venus and Cupid, who turned themselves into fish tied to a rope to escape the monster Typhon. In another version, as the gods and Titans warred, Aphrodite and her son Eros jumped into the Euphrates River to escape Typhon and were brought to safety by two fish. In another ending, they themselves became the fish.

The qualities of Pisces include being of two minds, servile, sociable, popular, and wandering. Pisces's selflessness can be seen in the fish that helped Aphrodite and Eros, and the gods' need to hide can also symbolize Pisces's wayward or inconsistent nature.

Further Considerations

One of the oldest determining features of signs and the planets is planetary rulership of the chart. This is ascertained by looking at the domicile rulership, the triplicity, the quadruplicity, exaltations and depressions, and the genders of the respective signs and planets. These various considerations all contribute to determining a chart's planetary ruler.

For instance, the domicile rulership (the "dwelling places" or "houses" of each planet) correlates with the genders of the signs and their connecting planetary rulers. The Sun and the Moon are the sect leaders of the masculine and feminine energies in astrology, respectively. In domicile rulership, the sign is completely at home, such as when the Moon is in Cancer or the Sun is in Leo.

Gender also plays a role: a masculine sign was viewed as more active, authoritative, and commanding, whereas the feminine signs were seen as more receptive, passive, and emotional. The remaining distinctions are the triplicity (or element) associated with the sign—Aries, for example, is connected to Fire, and Taurus is connected to Earth—and the quadruplicity, in which all signs are divided into one of three modalities: cardinal, fixed, and mutable.

PLANETARY RULERSHIP

Planetary rulership is an important concept that determines the exchange of power and other characteristics within a person's personality. There are four determinations associated with planetary rulership: the domicile or home, its detriment, its exaltation, and its fall. When a planet's position in the sign that it rules is in its rulership (or its home or domicile), the planet is able to fully utilize its qualities in a positive way. The Sun in Leo is in its rulership, so the positive qualities of the Sun will shine through. A Sun in Leo person can be naturally well-tempered, notable in some way, and intellectual.

On the other hand, when a planet is in the sign that is opposite its home or domicile, then the energy can be diffused or weakened, and the planet is in its detriment. For instance, the Sun in Aquarius, Leo's opposite sign, will cause the individual to lack a sense of ego and be single-minded and fearful.

The third feature is the exaltation, which is similar to domicile and is normally positive. The Sun is exalted in Aries, so the Sun can utilize the positive aspects of Aries, such as being authoritative, innovative, and bold.

The depression, or fall, is located in the sign opposite the exaltation sign (page 51). For instance, Libra is opposite to Aries, so it can dull the energy of that sign. A Sun in Libra individual can have a reduction in good and just thought or have trouble overseeing the balance in their life.

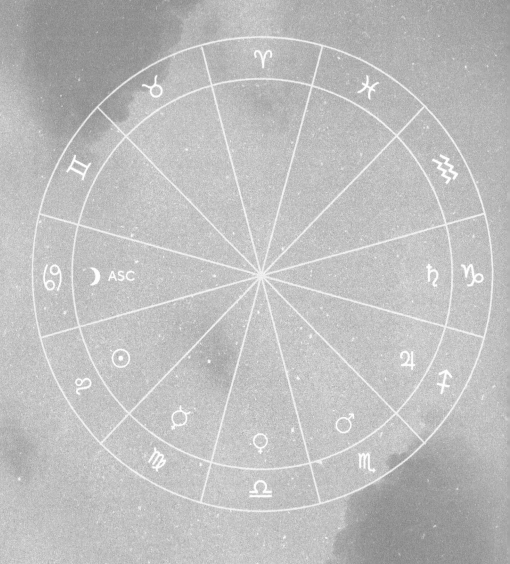

THE THEMA MUNDI

Thema Mundi is an ancient Greek term that means "World Theme" or "World Chart." It was used as a tool to understand the nuances and rationale for certain concepts in the astrological chart and ecliptic wheel.

There are a few versions of the Thema Mundi, but the earliest one, which originated in Egypt, has detailed the astrological placements of the Universe. It is said to depict the positions of the planets at the beginning of the Universe. Roman astrologer Firmicus Maternus referred to the work of Hermes Trismegistus by giving the below evidence of the Universe's astrological placements:

"They set up the birth chart of the universe as follows: the Sun in the fifteenth degree of Leo, the Moon in the fifteenth degree of Cancer, Saturn in the fifteenth degree of Capricorn, Jupiter in the fifteenth degree of Sagittarius, Mars in the fifteenth degree of Scorpio, Venus in the fifteenth degree of Libra, Mercury in the fifteenth degree of Virgo and the Ascendant in the fifteenth degree of Cancer."

DOMICILE RULERSHIP

Astrological signs each have a planetary correspondence, called a domicile or home, where they feel the most comfortable and are able to act most effectively and pull their strongest resources to the forefront. The Sun and the Moon, the sect leaders, are next to each other as the king (masculine) and the queen (feminine) of the zodiac, one lying above the horizon (Cancer), the other lying just below, ready to emerge and be "born" (Leo). This is where the assignment of domiciles begins, and from this, the other five planets fan out around the chart.

If one were to fold the Thema Mundi in half (page 48), with the Sun and Moon on opposite sides, the planetary connections for each of the remaining ten houses would be presented as a mirror effect.

The other five planets were granted two signs each, one feminine and one masculine.

The neighboring planet to the Sun and the Moon is Mercury, who is never more than one sign away from the Sun. Mercury was granted Gemini (masculine) and Virgo (feminine). Next comes Venus, who is never more than two signs away from the Sun. Venus was assigned Libra (masculine) and Taurus (feminine). After Venus, Mars was allocated Aries (masculine) and Scorpio (feminine). Jupiter was given Sagittarius (masculine) and Pisces (feminine). The opposite planet, Saturn, the most distant planet from the Sun and Moon, was given Aquarius (masculine) and Capricorn (feminine).

Planets in their domicile are viewed as being more positive or fortunate. They do not have to lean on other planets for support, and they will be "self-ruled" (*autodespota*) or "have their own power" (*autexousia*). For example, the Sun will be able to shine brilliantly in the sign of Leo. It feels "at home" here. A Sun in Leo person, without any other afflictions, will most likely be very confident, headstrong, and exuberant. Placing the Sun in another domicile, like Virgo, will reduce both the Leo and Virgo qualities, because neither planet nor sign feels "at home" with this placement. With the Sun in Virgo, rather than in domicile, a person might seem "uncomfortable" with who they are, resulting in a possibly cantankerous disposition. This also might produce a person who is a perfectionist, as the Sun characterizes one's identity and personality. This is where the ruler of their head lies.

GENDER

The masculine and feminine energies of a sign can signify various factors in an astrological chart. This determination can be divided among the elements with Fire (Aries, Sagittarius, and Leo) and Air (Gemini, Libra, and Aquarius) as masculine and Water (Cancer, Scorpio, and Pisces) and Earth (Taurus, Virgo, and Capricorn) as feminine.

The sect also plays a role in determining gender. For instance, the Sun's domicile is Leo, which is diurnal and masculine, whereas the Moon is domicile in Cancer, making it feminine and nocturnal, with the other five planets alternating both sect and gender. So, the next sign, Virgo, is nocturnal, then Libra is diurnal, Scorpio is nocturnal, Sagittarius is diurnal, Capricorn is nocturnal, Aquarius is diurnal, Pisces is nocturnal, Aries is diurnal, Taurus is nocturnal, and Gemini is diurnal.

In many cases, the most general definition of the gendered sign was connected to their masculine ("leading" or *hegemonias*) qualities, such as aggression and an active nature, or feminine ("subordination" or *hupotage*) qualities, such as passivity or an underactive nature.

EXALTATIONS AND DEPRESSIONS

The exaltation (*hupsoma*) shows the energy where a planet or sign can "rejoice" or exalt their qualities while being away from their domicile or home. The sign and planet can be exalted, but there are also specific degrees within this placement that are also exalted.

The Sun is exalted in Aries, which is also the start of the spring equinox, at 19 degrees, whereas the Moon is exalted in Taurus at 3 degrees.

Venus, on the other side of Aries, is exalted in Pisces at 27 degrees. Saturn in Libra, which holds the autumnal equinox, is exalted at 21 degrees. The neighboring sign, Virgo, is where Mercury is exalted at 15 degrees. Jupiter is exalted in Cancer at 15 degrees during the summer solstice. Mars is exalted in Capricorn, the sign opposite to Cancer, during the winter solstice at 28 degrees.

As mentioned on page 47, the depression (or fall) shows the energy where a planet or sign is weakened or dulled. This occurs in the sign opposite to the exaltation sign.

Dorotheus notes that the exaltation of the planet and sign shows where one can shine and be "illustrious and remarkable." In the *Michigan Papyrus*, an ancient Egyptian astrological manual, the exaltations are viewed as "thrones" or *thronous*, whereas the depressions are seen as "prisons" or *phulakas*.

TRIPLICITIES

The triplicities sort the twelve astrological signs into four sets of three signs, called trigons or triangles. These are based on the four elements (Fire, Air, Earth, and Water) and also on the four cardinal winds. The triplicity determines the energy of the element or wind that will be incorporated into the description of the sign. For instance, an individual with Jupiter in Leo during the day will associate with Fire and with the north wind and is ruled diurnally by the Sun. This person would exhibit strong leadership and authority.

The first triplicity holds the Fire element, the signs of Aries, Leo, and Sagittarius, and the north wind.

The second triplicity holds the Earth element, the signs of Taurus, Virgo, and Capricorn, and the south wind.

The third triplicity holds the Air element, the signs of Gemini, Libra, and Aquarius, and the east wind.

The fourth triplicity holds the Water element, the signs of Cancer, Scorpio, and Pisces, and the west wind.

Each triplicity is ruled by two planetary lords, one diurnal and one nocturnal, with a third lord that cooperates with the other two lords depending on the time of day. For instance, the first triplicity (Fire) is ruled by the Sun during the day and by Jupiter at night, and it cooperates with Saturn for both sects. For the second triplicity (Earth), Venus rules during the day and the Moon rules at night, with Mars cooperating with each planet. In the third triplicity (Air), Saturn rules during the day and Mercury rules in the evening, and Jupiter offers cooperation for both planets. Lastly, the fourth triplicity (Water) is ruled by Venus during the day and by Mars in the evening, with the Moon offering assistance for both.

Traditionally, the diurnal ruler represented the first part of one's life, the nocturnal ruler represented the second part, and the cooperating ruler represented the third part.

QUADRUPLICITIES

Quadruplicities, also called modalities in modern times, represent the three types of energies that groupings of four signs each can carry with them. These quadruplicities are fixed (*sterea* or solid), mutable (*disoma* or double-bodied), and cardinal (*tropika* or tropical).

Fixed energy signs Taurus, Leo, Scorpio, and Aquarius can make an individual doggedly stick to their ideas, tasks, or environments, for better or worse. Mutable Gemini, Virgo, Sagittarius, and Pisces can give a person two minds about a subject, making them indecisive or flighty. Cardinal Aries, Cancer, Libra, and Capricorn individuals can be very determined and focused but then lose interest just as quickly.

Ptolemy and Rhetorius understood that the traveling Sun showed the nature of these energies based on the season. For instance, as the Sun moves through the fixed signs, it is in the middle of a season and is steady and sure. Taurus is in the middle of spring, Leo is in the middle of summer, Scorpio is in the middle of fall, and Aquarius is in the middle of winter.

While moving through the cardinal signs, we are at the beginning of a season, with Aries in the spring, Cancer in the summer, Libra in the fall, and Capricorn in the winter. The Sun can be extremely sure about how it wants to be seen and what it wants to do; it is determined to go headfirst into the season.

Finally, as the Sun moves into the mutable signs of Gemini, Virgo, Sagittarius, and Pisces, the weather is unsure and ambiguous (or *epamphoteros*).

When we discuss the triplicities and quadruplicities, we see that the places (or houses) are associated with the diurnal rotation of the planets on the circular astrological wheel, as hour by hour the planets and signs rise, cross the sky, set, then spend the night below the horizon. The wheel of diurnal rotation was divided into twelve sections known as "places," "regions," or *topoi*. In the next chapter, we will discuss the twelve places in Hellenistic astrology.

CHAPTER 4

The Twelve Places

These twelve places of the zodiac address different areas of an individual's life, determine timing for an event, or give an understanding of the nature of a planet in this area.

Places are defined by the pie sections that make up the diurnal chart, whereas the houses are still determined by the signs. Only seven of the twelve places have corresponding planets that experience "joy" or a strong connection to the place: the Sun finds its joy in the ninth place, Jupiter finds its joy in the eleventh place, Saturn finds its joy in the twelfth place, Mercury finds its joy in the first place, the Moon finds its joy in the third place, Venus finds its joy in the fifth place, and Mars finds its joy in the sixth place.

Not all places have an attributed planet associated with them. Those that don't are the Midheaven or tenth place, the Gate of Hades or the second place, the Subterraneous or fourth place, the Setting or seventh place, and the Idle or eighth place.

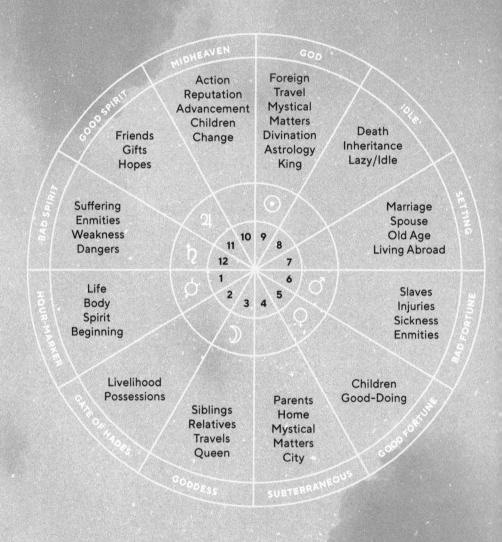

The Places Explained

The astrological places are numbered from one to twelve and appear in counterclockwise order on the circular diurnal rotation chart. The Ascendant or *anatellon*, which means "rising up," appears in the first place, also called the "Hour-Marker." The remaining eleven places continue onward from the first place and are each given a different name and characterization, which we will discuss further below.

The first place is called the Hour-Marker or Ascendant. The second place is the Gate of Hades (*Haidou pule*). The third place is the Goddess (*Thea*). The fourth place is Subterraneous (*hupogeion*). The fifth place is Good Fortune (*agathe tuche*), and the sixth place is Bad Fortune (*kake tuche*). The seventh place is Setting (*dusis*). The eighth place is Idle (*argos*). The ninth place is the God (*Theos*). The tenth place is the Midheaven (*mesouranema*). The eleventh place is Good Spirit (*Agathos Daimon*), and the twelfth place is Bad Spirit (*Kakos Daimon*).

There are distinctions between "good" and "bad" places. The former represents a connection to the positive aspects in one's life, such as children, family, friends, travel, and career, whereas the latter connects to the negative significations of loss, illness, and death. A place is "bad" when it brings a negative association or when it challenges the livelihood of the individual as addressed by the first place.

The four angles or pivots (*kentra*) are the first, fourth, seventh, and tenth places. They represent the foundation of the individual, and they goad the other planets into action. The places of decline (*apoklima*), moving away or falling from the pivots, are the third, sixth, ninth, and twelfth places. The succedent places (*epanaphora*), or those that follow after the pivots, are the second, fifth, eighth, and eleventh places.

Places are also seen as "busy" or *achrematisikos* (the four angles or the fifth, ninth, tenth, and eleventh places) and "advantageous" or *chrematisitkos* (the second, third, eighth, and twelfth places). Many astrologers have ranked the places from best to worst, starting with the first place, tenth, eleventh, fifth, seventh, fourth, ninth, second, third, eighth, sixth, and twelfth, respectively.

FIRST PLACE (HOUR-MARKER)

In Hellenistic astrology, the Hour-Marker is represented by the first house in the circular astrological chart. This first place is the first cardinal point and is ruled by Mercury, the neutral planet. Firmicus Maternus determined that the first place defines the life and vitality of an individual—their character and understanding of themself and how this is reflected to the outside world. Ancient astrologers, like Porphyry, believed that the soul enters the body through a "cosmic stream" or portal connected to the Ascendant at the time of birth.

Another name for the first place is the Helm, indicating that this is the first point of call when figuring out the idea of an individual and how others perceive them. The Hour-Marker is the starting point for the designation of places in the chart.

It is important to note that the first-place sign can be different from the Ascendant or Hour-Marker. For example, a Libra Ascendant marks the house of the Ascendant, whereas Saturn, as a ruling planet, can also be in the first place or rising when this person was born. Therefore, an individual will carry the qualities of both signs because they share the energy of the Hour-Marker or first place, the first impression that one makes on the world. In this example, this person will carry Libra traits, such as a strong connection to beauty and the arts, a diplomatic disposition, and a calm manner, but will also encompass the energy of Saturn, which may make them less optimistic and more sullen, or more serious-minded.

In fact, the faster-moving placements, the Ascendant, Moon, and Mercury, are more of a determining factor in who the individual is. Ptolemy in the *Tetrabiblos* states, "For indeed the differences between the signs which contain Mercury and the moon, or the planets that dominate them, can contribute much to the character of the soul." The soul represented the core personality of an individual and determined their key characteristics and traits. The Sun or the soul, which in modern astrology symbolizes the person and their ego, is actually more connected to the idea of the father, power, and the ability to shine in their field of choice.

SECOND PLACE (GATE OF HADES)

The second place in the astrological chart is called the Gate of Hades (*Haidou pule*), or the place of *bios* or "manner of living." This place is the succedent angle, meaning that it begins to move away from the sense of self, or Ascendant. As mentioned earlier, the meaning of the houses (the astrological signs) and the places in astrology have become intertwined. The ruler of each place, such as Aries for the first place and Aquarius for the eleventh place, was seen as carrying the qualities of that particular sign, which is not always the case.

In modern astrology, this house is normally associated with Taurus and material possessions. The second place is also connected to determining value within the things that we own, as well as our personal hopes, dreams, and self-worth.

The second place is called the Gate of Hades because it is completely cut off from the Helm, or the first place, and is considered to be a "bad" place (or *achrematisikos*). It is the last region that the planets travel through to get to the horizon, or Ascendant point, so it can be viewed to have a shadowy or hidden connection to the true life force, the first place. It is a passive place with no ruling planet guiding it around the zodiac.

An individual with a sign in the second place will be attempting to connect with value and abundance. For instance, Virgo in the second place can create someone who is a perfectionist when it comes to money, either not spending a dime or feeling guilty about spending money, believing that they might not have earned that right or have not worked hard enough. Therefore, they withhold themself from any form of material pleasure.

THIRD PLACE (GODDESS)

The third place is called the Goddess (*Thea*) and is ruled by the Moon, a nocturnal, benefic planet. The Moon has her joy here, so even though it is in decline, according to Rhetorius, it is considered to be a "good decline." This place also ends the move from the Earth triplicity into the Air triplicity of the third place.

It is the third sign from the Ascendant, beginning at 60 degrees from the Ascendant and stopping at 90 degrees. This is the place of short-distance travelers, siblings, dreams, divination, and relatives. The third place is connected to the Ascendant through a weak sextile aspect on the diurnal rotational wheel.

This is where the individual develops a sense of communication and "looks back" at the Ascendant place and sign through the lens of siblings or through their travels. The third place is seen as a "bad" place because it is not directly connected to the first place of the self and does not support the vitality and livelihood of the first place.

The third place is also where the Earth triplicity is in decline. The wheel is turning from Earth, representing the lower extremes of security and safety to one of instability, moving into the second house of the beginning Air triplicity or succedent place. This place can also be negatively associated with religion, worship, and sacred places. If afflicted in the chart, the individual can become blasphemous, lie, or "speak against the gods."

FOURTH PLACE (SUBTERRANEOUS)

The fourth place is connected with the Subterraneous (*hupogeion*) angle or underground place because it is at the bottom of the heavens in the chart. This place represents the second pivot angle or foundation of the individual. It is not ruled by a planet but serves as the connection between the succedent, or fifth place, and the decline, or third place, within the Earth triplicity in the diurnal rotation.

This connection to the Earth brings with it an association with the individual's foundation or roots. This cardinal place is also called

PLACES AND HOUSES

The places found in Hellenistic astrology are loosely connected to the houses found in modern astrology today. The term "houses" is taken from the concept of domicile in the zodiac, where a planet or sign feels "at home" in a certain area of the zodiac chart. Similar to the places in Hellenistic astrology, each house represents a different facet of our lives.

Valens in Book II of *Anthology* notes that when researching the areas of fortune or misfortune, the area that controls the "livelihood, life, injury, disease, occupation" within one's life can be ascertained by looking at the places/houses. The determination is constructed using opposing dichotomies within our lives, such as the self (first place/house), where we see issues with identity, versus the opposite, where we find marriage and partnership (seventh house/place), or looking at home and children (fifth place/house) versus the community or friends (eleventh place/house).

the Imum Coeli, beginning at 90 degrees and ending at 120 degrees. This is in opposition to the Medium Coeli, the Midheaven or the tenth place at the very top of the chart. As it is opposite the Midheaven, the most visible part of the chart, the Imum Coeli is considered to be hidden.

This place is represented by some of the "good" features of life, such as parents, the home, household possessions, family property, recovered wealth, mystical matters, the city life, and the house that the individual was born into. It is also the next place in the chart that, other than the first place, is "busy," which means that it goads the individual into acting on these pleasurable experiences and mindsets. This place is square with the Ascendant, making it a very powerful place.

The fourth place heavily influences the individual to act positively within the subjects connected to this place, which are family and the construction of a firm foundation of livelihood and the first place. The fourth place is also associated with old age, the end of life, funerals, and death. Because it is a "good" place, it does not carry a negative connection to these topics but an honest understanding that life includes death and that it can be dealt with in a more positive way, such as by the act of preparing for one's funeral.

FIFTH PLACE (GOOD FORTUNE)

The fifth place represents the second succedent place (or *epanaphora*), which follows after a pivot angle, the fourth place. Beginning at 120 degrees and ending at 150 degrees, it represents the place of children, sex, and positive experiences.

It is considered to be the place of Good Fortune (*agathe tuche*), especially as it is ruled by Venus, the planet of pleasure, beauty, love, and prosperity. Venus finds its joy in this place. Venus is a nocturnal planet and rejoices when it is below the horizon, as the fifth place is normally in the diurnal rotation chart.

This place forms a powerful aspect with the Ascendant and is in opposition to the Medium Coeli or Midheaven in the tenth place. It plays a large role in what makes an individual happy and prosperous. This place can be connected to a loss of personal assets through misfortune by not enacting the Venusian qualities of the fifth place, such as acts of benevolence, charity, and honor.

SIXTH PLACE (BAD FORTUNE)

The sixth place is the second decline place and is moving away from the pivot angle of the seventh house toward the succedent fifth house. The sixth place shows the movement on the diurnal rotation from the seventh place, which is a pivot angle to the Earth element triplicity. This can bring an aversion to the Ascendant place, the place of the self, and it is therefore viewed as going against the self.

It is 150 to 180 degrees from the Ascendant, meaning that it is not aspected to the Ascendant, the house of self and livelihood. This disconnection from the Ascendant place makes the sixth place an inactive, "bad," unfavorable, or disadvantageous place. It represents illness, sickness, enmities, and physical injuries within an individual's life. It is ruled by Mars, a nocturnal, malefic planet, which can bring harm and undoing to wherever it is placed. Consequently, this place is called the place of Bad Fortune.

If Saturn, a malefic planet, is found in this place, it can cause the individual to exhibit more of the qualities of the malefic planet rather than those of Venus, which is considered to be a benefic planet. Ptolemy gives an example of this: "If a place is allied with Venus in honourable positions [with] Saturn [this] makes his subjects haters of women, lovers of antiquity, solitary, unpleasant to meet, unambitious, hating the beautiful, envious, stern in social relations, not companionable, of fixed opinions, prophetic, given to the practice of religious rites, lovers of mysteries and initiations, and performers of sacrificial rites."

With Saturn aspecting Venus negatively and already in the "bad" house of Bad Fortune, the person will be a lover of all things considered negative, will hate women and those who are beautiful, and will love stern social relations and fixed opinions—anything that will not produce a positive outcome for the individual or their representation in the first place.

SEVENTH PLACE (SETTING)

The seventh place in the diurnal rotation is represented by the third pivot or angular house, the place of Setting. The place of Setting shows where the planets and stars go below the horizon, as opposed to where the planets, stars, and Ascendant rise. It is located 180 to 210 degrees from the first place, making it a cardinal point. It is also called the Descendant (*Dysis*) because it is opposite the first place, or Ascendant.

It is a key place in the life of an individual, as it forecasts marriage, the spouse, their old age, and the possibility of living abroad, which are major life changes for anyone. It is viewed as a "good" and advantageous place for a person to hold energy in. For instance, having multiple energies or planets in this place can mean that one will learn from love and from others, and this will reflect positively in their lives.

In modern astrology, this place would be associated with the sign Libra, whose main objective is to create union and harmony in relationships and to define a strong bond with the "other," which is a representation of the definition of this place. The seventh place is not ruled by a planet but is in the middle of the Water triplicity on the diurnal rotation. It is being pushed toward the Earth into the fifth house.

EIGHTH PLACE (IDLE)

The eighth place, or the Idle place, is also called *Epicatafora*, or the place "casting down into the underworld." It can be associated with laziness or not doing anything. It is a succedent angle, meaning that it is rising toward or following after a pivot, in this case the seventh place in the Water triplicity on the diurnal rotation.

It is located at 210 degrees and extends to 240 degrees away from the first place or the Ascendant. This makes it a passive or inactive house, as it is not in close aspect to the Ascendant. The eighth place represents death, inheritance, and idleness or laziness. It is not seen as a profitable house for the individual, especially as no planet rejoices here, except maybe the Moon in nocturnal charts.

Firmicus Maternus notes that if the Moon is waxing and is not afflicted by any other unfavorable planets, or if Jupiter is trine or sextile or is in the sign of Venus, Mercury, or Jupiter, "this portends the greatest good fortune and riches beyond measure, great glory of material power and outstanding recognition in worldly position." Even though this is not considered a "good" house, if the Moon were here, then the aspects connecting to this placement would grant the individual a happy livelihood of wealth and prosperity. This is an interesting concept, as this place in Western astrology is connected with the sign of Scorpio, which can be an intense, negative planet if afflicted.

NINTH PLACE (GOD)

The ninth place, or the place of God, is in its decline within the Fire element triplicity at the top of the diurnal rotation chart. The Sun rules this place, bringing with it prosperity, joyfulness, assertiveness, leadership qualities, strength, and versatility. The Sun has its joy in this place.

The "social class of men" is represented here as the individual, their position within society, their relation to others, their leadership status, and their higher calling. This place is also connected to religion and long-distance foreign travel, similar to the Western astrological connection to the sign of Sagittarius.

As this house is connected to the Sun god Helios, the bringer of light, who was said to have used his chariot to carry the Sun from the East to the West (page 23), this place asks the individual where they intend to bring their light to the world and how they intend to do so. Like the third place, the ninth place connects one to authority figures, such as kings and political leaders. This place also rules the head and thought, so the individual with this placement will be deciphering information and working to understand the nuances of subjects like foreign travel, astrology, mystical matters, philosophy, education, cults, and divination.

TENTH PLACE (MIDHEAVEN)

The Midheaven or Medium Coeli, also called "place at the peak" or the head (*koruphe*) or summit, is represented by the tenth place in the diurnal rotation. The tenth place does not have a planetary ruler, but it is a pivot angle, meaning that it represents key aspects for a sense of happiness and prosperity for the individual (the first place).

It is within 270 and 300 degrees away from the Ascendant, making it a square to the first place. It is also opposite the Subterraneous or fourth place, the Imum Coeli, where planets and the energy of those planets can become hidden and unused.

The Midheaven is at the very top of the horizon and is very visible, unlike the fourth place, or Imum Coeli, at the bottom of the chart. Ptolemy states that the Midheaven is the middle part of the Universe and represents our "vital spirit, all our actions, country, home, all our dealings with others, professional careers, and whatever our choice of career brings us." This is the place of *praxis*, or an action-oriented, "good," and advantageous place. The individual will be able to manifest a strong career, reputation, advancement, and positive change by focusing on the placements within the Midheaven or tenth place. One can learn a skill or trade and share it with others, thereby creating a good reputation.

It is interesting to note a difference from Western astrology here. As Hellenistic astrologers use the whole house sign system, the Midheaven may not always live in the tenth house as it is used today but can move to the ninth or eleventh houses, depending on which of the modern house systems are used.

ELEVENTH PLACE (GOOD SPIRIT)

The eleventh place or place of Good Spirit (*agathos daimon*) lies between 300 and 330 degrees from the Ascendant or first place. Moving from the Midheaven in the tenth place, the eleventh place is associated with the individual determining their dreams, hopes, and wishes and aspiring toward their strongest desires.

This place is also connected with friendships and alliances and becoming friends with powerful people in order to fulfill those goals. The eleventh place is a succedent place and follows the Midheaven, helping us see how to achieve these goals worked toward in the tenth place. Antiochus of Athens determined that it shows an "increase of things in the future" and the deliverance of gifts, acquisitions, honors, and dignity.

Jupiter, a benefic planet, rules this house and finds its joy here, bringing with it all of the positive qualities of the planet, such as prosperity, resourcefulness, joy, and strong connections. It is opposite the fifth house of children and Good Fortune, so this opposition can maximize the efforts of both places to bring prosperity into an individual's life.

TWELFTH PLACE (BAD SPIRIT)

The twelfth place, or place of Bad Spirit (*kakos daimon*), is the decline angle of the Hour-Marker, or Ascendant. It is ruled by the malefic planet Saturn, which brings with it sorrow, melancholy, and misfortune. It rises just before the individual's birth, making it, as Brennan says, a "place between worlds." Rhetorius notes that this place of limbo, which represents the underworld, is an area that encompasses "everything that happens before the moment of the native's birth, both for the mother and the child, since this sign rises prior to the separation of the two."

The individual can sometimes feel the negative influences that occurred before they were born, such as divorce, family arguments, poverty, or trauma. The twelfth place is also associated with enemies and those who are weakened within society, linking this place to suffering, pain, ailments, injuries, weakness, and death.

This is a place of passivity or inaction, as the native might be weary or browbeaten from negative occurrences before and during life. Saturn finds its joy here and brings all of its qualities to this place, such as sullenness, a predisposition to silence, depression, anxiety, sorrow, grief, lack of emotional display, and inaction. It is also connected to four-legged animals, difficult travel, or banishment from one's country.

The Places and the Planets

Most of the twelve places are connected to a planet that can find its "joy" or exaltation, a place where the strong qualities of the planet can be rejoiced within it. Mercury finds its joy in the first place, the Moon in the third, Venus in the fifth, Mars in the sixth, the Sun in the ninth, Jupiter in the eleventh, and Saturn in the twelfth.

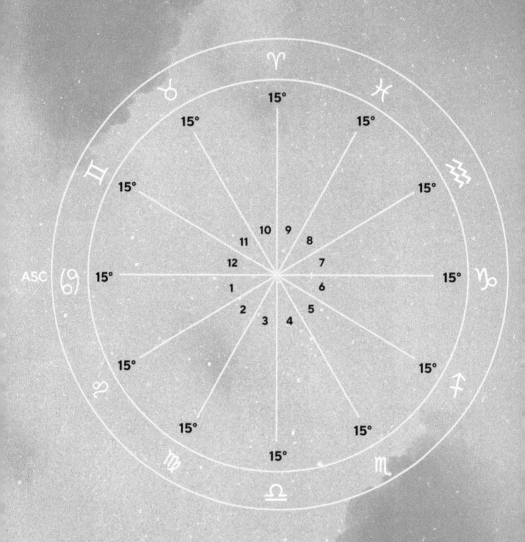

THE HOUSE SYSTEMS

In Hellenistic astrology, the whole house system was the most used method of determining the places/houses in the zodiac chart. There were three different techniques used to create a chart: the whole house system, the equal house system, and the quadrant house system.

For the whole house system, once the rising sign is identified, one can count the other eleven houses to each sign so that each house/place has a sign of 30 degrees that it begins and ends with, known as the "cusp."

The equal house system starts with the degree of the Ascendant and counts 30 degrees forward, counterclock- wise, to determine the next sign and house/place. So if the first house starts at 15 degrees Libra, the next one will be 15 degrees Scorpio, then 15 degrees Sagittarius, and so on.

In the quadrant house system, you determine the degrees of opposite placements, the Ascendant and Descendant, and then the Midheaven (tenth place) and the Imum Coeli (fourth place) separately. This will divide the chart into four equal sections, then each of those four sections are divided into three equal sections.

When we look at the planet and the place in terms of deciphering joy or exaltation, we look at both the associations and qualities of the place and the qualities of the planet, and vice versa. For example, the Sun in the seventh place can symbolize that the individual can marry someone who has characteristics and traits that mirror the individual's father. The seventh place shows our connection to the father figure and the facets of their character. The individual can marry a spouse who shares these characteristics.

Likewise, the planet can also show us the type of action that needs to occur. Venus in the twelfth place can show an individual having relationships or a strong connection to those who could be restrained in some way, physically or psychologically, such as those in prison, a person with mental health issues, or someone who lives far away in a foreign land.

Due to the multiple associations with the places, the individual can encounter multiple instances within that place or they can encounter only one. For example, the individual referenced above with Venus in the twelfth place can at one point have a relationship with someone in jail. At another point, they might feel constrained or isolated within a relationship, making the individual feel like a prisoner in the relationship.

Making Sense of Placements

The connection of planets, signs, and the qualities of the places comes from the term "witnessing" or testimony. The ancient Greek word is *epimartuia*, defined by Antiochus and Porphyry of Tyre. The qualities of the planets within a diurnal or nocturnal chart in relation to a benefic or malefic planet are important determining factors of what the planet signifies in one's chart.

If an individual has one of the diurnal planets—the Sun, Mars, or Jupiter—in a place above the horizon, this is seen as a positive connection to both the attributes of the planet and those of the place. Similarly, if a benefic or malefic planet is placed in a benefic or malefic place, this can also color the attributes of the individual's response to the sign.

For instance, if Saturn, a malefic planet, is placed in a malefic place, such as the sixth place, this will double the negative associations with both the planet and the place, making the individual sullen and melancholy, possibly when they are at work. On the other hand, this emotion might make them feel perpetually ill or mentally unwell.

Saturn in the twelfth place seems very bad, as both the planet and house are malefic. Saturn finds its joy in the twelfth, however, and the result will not be as disastrous for the individual. If there are positive aspects to this house, they will be able to find a way out of the negative attributes associated with these houses.

The movements of the seven wandering stars, the twelve places, and the twelve astrological signs through the diurnal rotation zodiac comprise a large role in understanding and deciphering one's astrological chart in Hellenistic astrology. The next important facet of chart interpretation is the lots, which are mathematical points that offer additional information outside of the places and signs. We'll discuss these in the following chapter.

CHAPTER 5

The Lots

One of the cornerstones of chart interpretation in Hellenistic astrology is the lots, or *kleroi*. Lots are not attributed to a particular planet, astrological sign, or aspect. They are instead calculated mathematical points derived from the positions of other placements in the zodiac. The lots give additional information about the astrological zodiac chart that cannot be determined from the subjects of the twelve places.

In modern day astrology, the lots are referred to as "Arabic parts." Brennan notes that the term Arabic parts is a "misnomer, however, as the Medieval Arabic tradition of astrology only began around 775 CE, while this technique had already been in use in the Greco-Roman astrological tradition since at least first century BCE." Whereas Greek Hellenistic astrologers attributed the original seven Hermetic lots to each of the seven wandering stars, Arabic astrologers added many more lots, expanding from the original concept derived from the Greeks, granting them the credit and namesake of the lots in modern astrology.

In this chapter, we will learn about the seven Hermetic lots of Hellenistic astrology, their planetary associations and how to calculate them.

Calculating a Lot

Cleromancy, or the art of "casting" or "drawing" lots, was a divinatory practice of interpreting and deciding on an outcome from "chance" or through the will of the gods. This practice dates back to the start of Hellenistic astrology, around the third century BCE.

Astrologer Dorian Gieseler Greenbaum notes that the casting of lots was embedded in Greek mythology and history. She states that in the *Iliad*, "even the gods cast lots to make decisions: the allotments of the portions of the world land to Zeus, Poseidon and Hades were made by lot." The most precise method for calculating a lot is to first measure the distance or longitude of the Ascendant (A) by counting the number of degrees, and then add (+) the distance or longitude (again, counting the degrees in between) of the first planet or point (B), and then subtract (-) the longitude (counting the degrees in between) of the second planet or point (C), which will look like this:

$$A + B - C = Lot$$

In Hellenistic texts, the casting of the lots was different for day (diurnal) and night (nocturnal) charts, which were instead calculated by interpreting the distance between the Sun, Moon, and Ascendant. It was also important to take note of the order of the zodiac signs, because in diurnal charts, the Sun moves toward the Moon, whereas in nocturnal charts, the Moon moves toward the Sun.

When calculating the Lot of Fortune, for diurnal charts, we measure the distance from the Sun to the Moon (A), then use that same distance (A) and measure it from the Ascendant. In nocturnal charts, we measure the distance from the Moon to the Sun (B) and then use that same distance (B) and measure it from the Ascendant. The resulting sign and degree where this falls in the zodiac chart is the Lot of Fortune.

Day ☉: Sun - Moon (A) + (A) Ascendant = Lot of Fortune (diurnal)
Night ☽: Moon - Sun (B) + (B) Ascendant = Lot of Fortune (nocturnal)

Analyzing a Lot

All calculations in Hellenistic astrology were completed by calcu-lating the distance from one point to the next and then counting the same distance from the Ascendant, or first place. One takes into con-sideration the place and sign that the Moon, Sun, and Ascendant are in to fully grasp the position of the lot. Analysis of these calculations becomes possible after determining the measurements of a lot.

For example, let's calculate the lot for someone with a diurnal chart: Sun in Cancer at 10 degrees, Moon in Aries at 3 degrees, and Scorpio Ascendant at 4 degrees.

Moving clockwise from the position of the Sun sign, Cancer in the ninth place at 10 degrees, to the Moon in Aries in the sixth place at 3 degrees, we get a measurement of 97 degrees. Still moving clockwise, we then take the 97 degrees and measure out this same distance from the Ascendant in Scorpio at 4 degrees, and we get the lot as Cancer at 27 degrees in the ninth place.

If we were calculating a nocturnal chart for that same person, we would move in a counterclockwise fashion in calculating the distance from the Moon to the Sun, resulting in 260 degrees. Moving that many degrees away from the Ascendant point, we get the lot as Aries at 23 degrees in the sixth place.

In analyzing the diurnal result of the lot in the first example, Cancer at 27 degrees in the ninth place, we can ascertain that this individual will find positive interactions with this placement. The ninth place (God), is ruled by the Sun, a benefic planet in a "good" place, so there brings prosperity concerning foreign travel, divina-tion, and association with authority figures. With the sign of Cancer, this person could be a supportive influence to these authority figures or could help others manifest this within their lives. Cancer and the Moon are positively connected to the Sun and Leo, which also reside in the opposing energy of the third place (Goddess) of siblings, travel, and communication.

When analyzing the nocturnal result of the lot of Aries in the sixth place, that same person will see a negative influence, as the sixth place is malefic, and Aries, ruled by Mars, is also the lord of the sixth place. The individual might have to deal with injuries or illnesses, but because Aries is in a place with its original lord Mars, the effects can be overcome.

CALCULATING THE LOTS FOR DIURNAL AND NOCTURNAL CHARTS

When calculating the lots for both diurnal and nocturnal charts, take into account that each place, or section of the chart, is made up of 30 degrees. When counting backward or forward, remember that each place moves from 0 to 30 degrees in a clockwise fashion.

When completing a diurnal chart, make sure to remember to count backward from that degree (i.e., 27 degrees Aries is not the same as 3 degrees Aries). For nocturnal charts, we move in a counterclockwise fashion, always starting from the Moon and moving toward the Sun. Similarly, when calculating diurnal charts, we move in a clockwise fashion, always starting from the Sun and moving toward the Moon.

This will make it easier to determine the lots differently between diurnal and nocturnal charts. It is good to practice both methods as various lots specifically utilize the diurnal or nocturnal method, or both, to calculate their lots. For instance, the Lot of Fortune moves both diurnally and nocturnally but is meant to calculate the lot for the Sun sign. The Lot of Spirit moves in a nocturnal fashion, counterclockwise, and is meant to calculate the lot for the Moon sign.

The Seven Hermetic Lots

Now that we understand how to calculate and analyze the lots, let us determine the various types of lots. The seven Hermetic lots became widely used through the efforts of Paul of Alexandria, an astrologer in the fourth century CE. He determined the use of lots from the work *Panaretus*, which is attributed to Hermes Trismegistus, one of the founders of Hellenistic astrology.

Each of the seven lots correlate with one of the seven wandering stars and have different calculations. The Lot of Fortune is associated with the body and livelihood (the Moon), whereas the Lot of Spirit is linked to the soul and intellect (the Sun). Both lots are neutral.

The Lot of Eros (correlated with Venus) and the Lot of Victory (Jupiter) have positive affiliations. The malefic planets, Mars and Saturn, and their Lot of Courage and Lot of Nemesis, respectively, as well as Mercury's Lot of Necessity, can hold negative connotations. These lots determine the role that different occurrences will have in one's life, in accordance to the benefic or malefic energy of the planet and place.

LOT OF FORTUNE

According to Valens, the Lot of Fortune is the "archetypal lot." It is used by all Hellenistic astrologers to determine one of the core underlying concepts of Hellenistic astrology, the notion of fate and determinism. Many ancient astrologers believed that if an individual has a well-situated Lot of Fortune with connections to a benefic place, planet, or sign, then they will still have a chance at having a successful and happy life despite malefic representations in their chart.

The Lot of Fortune is connected with the Moon, the body (*soma*), one's livelihood (*tas kata bion praxeis*), marriage, reputation, appearance, gains, and possessions, as well as how they conceive or create. Valens writes, "For cosmically the Moon is fortune and body and breath, and since she is close to the earth and sends her effluence into us, she brings about something similar as she has authority over our body."

As the Moon is the closest "sublunary sphere" to Earth, it is viewed, according to Greenbaum, as "the boundary between heaven and Earth." The Lot of Fortune is a neutral lot, meaning that although it does not add benefic or malefic energy within the lot itself, it can add those as a result of determining the sign or place where the lot is found. The best way to remember the calculations for the Lot of Fortune is that there should be the same number of degrees between the Sun and the Moon as there is between the Ascendant and the Lot of Fortune.

Interestingly, the Lot of Fortune, as Brennan notes, "is always determined by starting from the luminary that is of sect in favor, otherwise known as the 'sect light,' and then counting the distance to the luminary that is contrary to the sect in favor." So, for instance, as the Moon is associated with the Lot of Fortune, the calculation to determine this lot, moving from the Sun to the Moon in diurnal charts and the Moon to the Sun in nocturnal charts, shows that we are moving from the sect leader (the Sun) to the sect light (the Moon) during the day, and from the sect leader (the Moon) to the sect light (the Sun) in the evening.

With the Lot of Fortune, which is connected to the Moon and therefore the body, we move from light to darkness. This underlies the Hermetic theme of "darkness being associated with matter and physical incarnation." In the Lot of Fortune, we are moving toward our actions in the physical sense and toward what we do and accomplish in life.

Day ☉: Sun - Moon (A) + (A) Ascendant = Lot of Fortune (diurnal)
Night ☽: Moon - Sun (B) + (B) Ascendant = Lot of Fortune (nocturnal)

LOT OF SPIRIT

The Lot of Spirit, also called the "Lot of Daimon" or fate, is connected to the Sun and to our intellect (*phronesis*), temper, authority, leadership, dealings with the gods, fortune, and to the father and key notable figures of power (*dunasteia*) in our lives. We can also use this lot to determine the best occupation for an individual, spurring them into action.

Valens adds that "the Sun, which is cosmically mind and daimon on account of his own activity and lovely nature, stirring up human souls for undertakings, is established as a cause of action and movement." In short, this means that the Sun, by its very nature, spurs us into action and purpose. Similar to the Lot of Fortune and its connection with lightness and darkness, the Lot of Spirit is connected to the Sun, the mind, and intellect. The calculation to determine this lot, moving from the Moon to the Sun in diurnal charts and the Sun to the Moon in nocturnal charts, shows that we are moving from the sect leader (the Moon) to the sect light (the Sun) during the day and from the sect leader (the Sun) to the sect light (the Moon) in the evening.

Again, here we are moving from darkness to light. Relating back to Hermetic or Gnostic theology, the pursuit of the mind and the intellect was of a "higher" or "more noteworthy" pursuit in one's life, more so than that of fortune, although both are valued as part of fate.

The calculation to determine the Lot of Spirit will look like this:

Day ☉: Moon - Sun + Ascendant = Lot of Spirit (diurnal)
Night ☽: Sun - Moon + Ascendant = Lot of Spirit (nocturnal)

Rhetorius gives an example of Jupiter (Zeus) located in the Lot of Spirit (or Daimon): "When Zeus is beholding the Lot of Daimon, such a one receives divine revelation from gods and dreams and will have all divine favors." This person will be given the luck of being able to divine and connect with spirts through their dreams.

LOT OF EROS

The planet Venus, or the "light bringer," holds jurisdiction over the Lot of Eros. Eros is the name for the Greek god of sexual desire, love, and companionship. The Romans knew him as Cupid. In ancient Greek history, love or Eros was viewed as a "guide," a "savior," or a "physician," unencumbered with the messy details of life, pain, and suffering but connected to the soul, which fills us corporeally and spiritually.

Venus signifies divine love, the nurse, the mother, royal women and relatives, laughter, rejoicing, marriage, beauty of form, art, friendship, desires, appetites, and favor. To calculate the Lot of Eros, you must first calculate the Lot of Spirit.

For day charts, the Lot of Eros is calculated by measuring the distance from the Lot of Spirit to the planet Venus and then applying that measurement from the Ascendant. For night charts, the Lot of Eros is calculated by measuring the distance from the planet Venus to the Lot of Spirit and applying that measurement from the Ascendant.

Day ☉: Lot of Spirit - Venus + Ascendant = Lot of Eros (diurnal)
Night ☽: Venus - Lot of Spirit + Ascendant = Lot of Eros (nocturnal)

LOT OF NECESSITY

Mercury rules the Lot of Necessity (or *Ananke*). According to ancient Hellenistic astrologers, Necessity or *Ananke* is seen as the "axis of the cosmos." Necessity is said to be born from the theology of the first principles, Earth and Water. From there, Kronos (Saturn) and Necessity (Mercury) were born.

Necessity is seen as duplicitous or having two sides. This is, as Greenbaum notes, evidence of Necessity being both male and female "as a sign that she was the cause of bringing all things to birth." The ability to carry both male and female characteristics is synonymous with the description of Mercury.

Similarly, Necessity, according to Greenbaum, is also known to represent a "firm decision and unalterable power of Providence," with both Necessity and Order as unswayable parts of "God's divine plan." Mercury rules over education, knowledge, brotherhood, writing, mathematics, youthfulness, community, service, sending messages, critical thinking, judgment, builders, augurs, and dream interpreters.

Mercury is also said to connect with constraints, subordinations or subjections, wars, enemies, condemnations, and battles. In order to calculate the Lot of Necessity, one must know their Lot of Fortune, which is ruled by the Moon. For diurnal charts, measure Mercury to the Lot of Fortune, and for nocturnal charts, measure the Lot of Fortune to Mercury.

Day ☉: Lot of Fortune - Mercury + Ascendant = Lot of Necessity (diurnal)
Night ☽: Mercury - Lot of Fortune + Ascendant = Lot of Necessity (nocturnal)

LOT OF COURAGE

The planet Mars, or Ares, "the fiery one," presides over the Lot of Courage. Rhetorius states that the Lot of Courage "is indicative of boldness, plotting, strength and every evil work" or evildoing (*kakourgias*), violence, adultery, rape, captivity, sexual intercourse, loss of good things, hopeless situations, hatred, lawsuits, bloodshed, masculinity, skin eruptions, deception, leaders, the military, hunting, regalia, and poor vision.

To calculate the Lot of Courage, one must know their Lot of Fortune. These two emotional lots can find their connection through the body (the Moon) and physicality (Mars). Both planets and lots determine how treacherous, strong, emotionally passionate, and bold someone can be in this life. For diurnal charts, one measures from Mars to the Lot of Fortune and then from the Ascendant. For nocturnal charts, you calculate from the Lot of Fortune to Mars and then from the Ascendant.

Day ☉: Mars - Lot of Fortune + Ascendant = Lot of Courage (diurnal)
Night ☽: Lot of Fortune - Mars + Ascendant = Lot of
Courage (nocturnal)

LOT OF VICTORY

Jupiter, or Zeus, "the radiant one," rules over the Lot of Victory. This lot symbolizes faith, contests, good hope, generosity, success, knowledge, begetting children, desire, love, alliances, governments, justice, abundance, honor, inheritances, relief from bad things, freedom, fellowship, and adoption.

According to Paul of Alexandria and Olympiodorus the Younger, an astrologer in the sixth century CE, "Victory becomes responsible for faith, good expectation, contest and every kind of association, but it becomes as well responsible for penalty and reward." In "Orphic Hymns to Eros, Tyche, and Daimon," Zeus is seen as the "grand and dreaded leader" showing that he can be revered or feared; he is "laden with goods" and can "drive painful cares away," especially the life-destroying ones:

"I call upon Daimon, the grand and dreaded leader, gentle Zeus, who gives birth to all and livelihood to mortals; great Zeus, wide roving, avenger, king of all, giver of wealth when you enter the house, laden with goods, you refresh the life of mortals worn out with toil. You possess the keys to joy and sorrow as well. So, O pure and blessed one, drive painful cares away, cares that are life-destroying throughout the whole earth, and bring a glorious, sweet and noble end to life."

By day, Zeus and the planet Jupiter allow the individual to determine their Lot of Victory by measuring the Lot of Spirit to Jupiter and then from the Ascendant. By night, you would measure from Jupiter to the Lot of Spirit and then from the Ascendant.

Day ☉: Lot of Spirit - Jupiter + Ascendant = Lot of Victory (diurnal)
Night ☽: Jupiter - Lot of Spirit + Ascendant = Lot of Victory (nocturnal)

LOT OF NEMESIS

The Lot of Nemesis is linked to the planet Saturn, or Kronos. Kronos was said to be one of the original offspring of Earth and Water, "born," as Greenbaum says, "with the heads of a bull and a lion with god's face in the middle." Rhetorius determines that "Kronos's Lot—the Lot of Nemesis—is established [as responsible for] earthly daimons, all hidden things, [their] exposure, insolence, exile, destruction, grief and the quality of death." Similarly, Paul of Alexandria adds that Nemesis is also aligned with exposure, impotence, exile, loss, mourning, and the quality of death.

The planet Saturn, also referred to as "the shining one," rules over anxiety, squalor, black clothes, misery, depression, seafaring waysides, long punishments, accusations, tears, captivity, exposure, spirit possession, childishness, widows, and violent deaths. This lot can also be referred to as the Lot of Retribution, with a focus on the underworld and anything hidden.

The Lot of Nemesis is calculated by first determining the Lot of Fortune. For a diurnal chart, one would measure from Saturn to the Lot of Fortune and then measure from the Ascendant. For a nocturnal chart, you would measure from the Lot of Fortune to Saturn and then measure from the Ascendant.

Day ☉: Saturn - Lot of Fortune + Ascendant = Lot of Nemesis (diurnal)
Night ☽: Lot of Fortune - Saturn + Ascendant = Lot of Nemesis (nocturnal)

LOTS AND THE FOUR DEITIES

The earlier formulas for the seven Hermetic lots came from the works of Paul of Alexandria in the fourth century CE. His contributions can be seen in the works of many philosophers and astrologers between the fourth and fifth centuries CE as a cornerstone of Greek religion and human civilization.

For instance, in his books the *Commentary on Cicero's Dream of Scipio* and the *Saturnalia*, Macrobius discusses the zodiac, astrology, and the planets in relation to the "genesis" of mankind:

"[. . .] for they say that four deities are present to preside over a man's birth: his Daimōn, Tuchē, Erōs and Anankē [Daimon, Fortune, Love and Necessity]. By the first two they understand the sun and the moon; for the sun, as the source of the breath of life and of heat and of light, is the creator and the guardian of a man's life and is therefore believed to be the daimon, or god, of a new born child; the moon is Tuchē [Fortune], since she has charge of the body, and the body is at the mercy of the fickleness of change; the kiss of the serpents is the symbol of Love; and the knot is the symbol of Necessity."

The four deities that Macrobius mentions are seen as significant qualifiers not only in the astrological world but also in Hellenistic philosophy and religion. The Lots of Spirit (body) and Fortune (mind, soul) are linked to the Lots of Eros (love) and Necessity (the cosmos) as represented by the "four deities" within the caduceus, "which preside over a man's birth."

Additional Lots

As the study of Hellenistic astrology has gone through various incarnations and interpretations, this section will detail the alternate formulas used to calculate the Lot of Necessity, which was already mentioned, in addition to new lots: the Lots for Family Members, Death, Illness, Accusation, Exaltation, and Foundation. Ancient astrologers in the second century CE, such as Dorotheus, Valens, and Firmicus, worked with an earlier representation of calculations for the Lot of Necessity as listed in this section.

LOT OF NECESSITY

Unlike the connection between the first Lot of Necessity and the planet Mercury, the second Lot of Necessity is not linked to a planet. The Lot of Necessity, according to Valens in Book II, chapter 16 of *Anthology*, is associated with enemies (*echtron*). In ancient Greek philosophy, "Necessity," according to Greenbaum, "is a goddess in the Purifications, she is associated with oracles and oaths, and seems to be very ancient: 'There is an oracle of Necessity, a decree of the gods long ago, eternal and sealed by broad oaths.'"

This connection to Necessity as a purifier and manager of oaths taken and broken seems to relate to the idea that enemies can be formed when ties and oaths are broken. This Lot of Necessity describes the nature and focus of competition, disputes, and challenges in the individual's life. Depending on if it is in contact with malefic or benefic planets or places, it will bring either victory and success or failure.

Day ☉: Lot of Spirit - Lot of Fortune + Ascendant = Lot of Necessity (diurnal)

Night ☽: Lot of Fortune - Lot of Spirit + Ascendant = Lot of Necessity (nocturnal)

LOTS FOR THE FAMILY MEMBERS

One of the added lots in the Arabic tradition are the Lots of Family Members, including those for the Father, Mother, Siblings, Marriage, and Children. The Lot of the Father is associated with the Sun and the planet Saturn. Both planets are masculine, diurnal, and connected with children. The former is viewed as a more positive representation of the father, of kingly authority, benevolence, intelligence, and nobility, whereas the latter represents the negative connections of the "father figure," such as pettiness, deceitfulness, misery, control, captivity, and violence. The Lot of the Father is calculated using the positions of the Sun, Saturn, and the Ascendant:

Day ☉: Sun - Saturn + Ascendant = Lot of the Father (diurnal)
Night ☽: Saturn - Sun + Ascendant = Lot of the Father (nocturnal)

The Lot of the Mother is calculated using Venus, the Moon, and the Ascendant. Both the Moon and Venus are nocturnal benefic planets associated with women in one's family, as well as femininity, receptiveness, marriage, beauty, the goddess, and the appearance. This is the calculation for the Lot of the Mother:

Day ☉: Venus - Moon + Ascendant = Lot of the Mother (diurnal)
Night ☽: Moon - Venus + Ascendant = Lot of the Mother (nocturnal)

The Lot of Siblings, also called the Lot of Brothers (which in ancient Greek terminology can refer to siblings of both sexes), uses the planets Saturn and Jupiter in its calculations. This is the only lot where the same formula is used for both the diurnal and the nocturnal charts.

Saturn - Jupiter + Ascendant = Lot of the Siblings

The Lot of Marriage is calculated with the planets Saturn and Venus. Dorotheus and Paul of Alexandria believed that one should have a different measurement for females and males, with the former calculated by measuring Venus to Saturn and then the Ascendant, and the latter calculated by measuring from Saturn to Venus and then the Ascendant. To contrast, Firmicus felt that this formula should only be used for males with the day and night formulas, with the latter calculation for the day and the former calculation for the night. Firmicus believed that females have a separate calculation for the Lot of Marriage, which measures the distance from Mars to Venus by day and then reverses it for the evening.

Females / Night ☽: Venus - Saturn + Ascendant = Lot of
Marriage (diurnal/nocturnal)
Males / Day ☉: Saturn - Venus + Ascendant = Lot of
Marriage (nocturnal/diurnal)

There are other "Arabic parts" of Marriage, such as the Lots of Pleasure and Wedding, which have the same formula for day and night, calculated from Venus to the "degree of the seventh sign" and then the same distance from the Ascendant. The Lot of Wedding, which also has the same day and night formula, is measured from the Sun to the Moon. That measurement is then calculated from the degree of Venus for males and Mars for females, measuring the same distance from the seventh sign degree. The use of Venus for men is connected to the idea that in a chart you look to Venus for a man's spouse and Mars for a female's spouse.

The Lot of Children is the opposite of the Lot of Siblings. According to Dorotheus and Paul of Alexandria, it is determined by calculating from Jupiter to Saturn and then the distance from the Hour-Marker for both diurnal and nocturnal charts. Valens differentiates between genders—the Lot of Brothers for the male and the Lot of Daughters for the female. The former is calculated by measuring the distance from Jupiter to Mercury, then applying it to the Ascendant, whereas the latter is calculated by measuring the distance from Jupiter to Venus and then applying it to the Ascendant.

LOT OF DEATH

The Lot of Death has come from places outside of ancient Greece. Hephaestion of Thebes references Dorotheus in noting that this calculation is created by measuring from the Moon to the eighth sign from the Ascendant, or the eighth whole sign place from the Hour-Marker, and then measuring that resulting distance from the planet Saturn. The place, sign, and planets involved could let us know how the individual dies.

Day ☉/Night ☽: Moon - Eighth Sign from the Ascendant + Saturn
= Lot of Death (diurnal/nocturnal)

LOT OF ILLNESS/ACCUSATION

The Lot of Illness or Accusation is determined by using the planets Saturn and Mars, two malefics. For the day, one will measure the distance from Saturn to Mars and then calculate from the Ascendant. Reverse this formula for the evening. The sign that the lot falls in will symbolize where the individual will develop a chronic illness.

For instance, as the Sun is synonymous with the torso and the heart, Rhetorius describes how "the Sun obtaining (as his portion) the Lot of Injury makes cardiac injuries." Similarly, Valens gives a description of the bodily afflictions and illnesses ruled by each place in the zodiac:

Some, then, who focus their attention on the affected places of the body and the soul, making, for each person's nativity, the beginning of the [assignment of] body parts from the Lots of Fortune and Daimon, present the place of injury and illness in reference to the presence of malefics. [. . .] The illnesses [are] from the [Lot] of Daimon, for the Daimon itself is the heart, the 2nd zodiac sign [from it] the innards, the 3rd that through which the sperm is carried and place of the kidneys, the 4th the colon, the 5th the liver, the 6th the second belly [the womb?], the 7th the bladder, the 8th the intestines, the 9th the place of membranes, teeth and ears, the 10th the gullet, the 11th the tongue, the 12th the stomach.

Day ☉: Saturn - Mars + Ascendant = Lot of Illness/Accusation (diurnal)
Night ☽: Mars - Saturn + Ascendant = Lot of Illness/Accusation (nocturnal)

LOT OF EXALTATION

The Lot of Exaltation can be connected to one's career path, talent, professional skills, and where they can be best recognized in terms of social status. The Lot of Exaltation uses the distance from the Sun and the Moon to two signs of the zodiac, Aries and Taurus. One measures the distance from the sect light to the sign of its exaltation (Aries or Taurus), paying attention to the location of the lords of domicile of the place.

For instance, the Lot of Exaltation in the ninth place may symbolize someone who travels for a living, such as a trader or salesman, a pilot or flight attendant, or even possibly an astrologer or diviner. For diurnal charts, measure the distance from the Sun to Aries and then measure the same distance from the Ascendant. For nocturnal charts, measure the distance from the Moon to Taurus, then the same distance from the Ascendant.

Day ☉: Sun - Aries + Ascendant = Lot of Exaltation (diurnal)
Night ☽: Moon - Taurus + Ascendant = Lot of Exaltation (nocturnal)

LOT OF FOUNDATION/BASIS

The Lot of Foundation or Basis, also called "the Hour-Marker's Lot," provides a strong connection between the Lot of Fortune (the Moon and the body) and the Lot of Spirit (the Sun and the mind). The Lot of Foundation/Basis shows us how to maintain the fortune that we have acquired. It also shows us how we "turn the key" or allow the good fortune of the Lot of Spirit to befall us.

Therefore, to determine this lot, one must first calculate the Lots of Fortune and Spirit. Using these calculations, one can measure the shortest distance from the Lot of Fortune to the Lot of Spirit for diurnal charts, and for nocturnal charts, measure the shortest distance from the Lot of Spirit to the Lot of Fortune. Brennan notes that by focusing on the shortest distance, one has the free will to determine between Eros and Necessity.

The Lot of Foundation/Basis is always found below the horizon of the zodiac chart, connecting its namesake with the grounding energy needed to enact change in one's life (similar to the fourth place, which is found at the bottom of the chart and is associated to one's foundations and roots in life). Rhetorius states, "The Hour-marker's Lot—the Lot of Basis—is established as responsible for life and breath; for Basis itself is the giver of breath for the *hōroskopos*, and signifies bodily things and living abroad," meaning that the first place, or the Ascendant, and the fourth place are inextricably linked to each other on the basis of life.

Day ☉: Lot of Fortune - Lot of Spirit + Ascendant = Lot of Foundation/Basis (diurnal)

Night ☽: Lot of Spirit - Lot of Fortune + Ascendant = Lot of Foundation/Basis (nocturnal)

Besides the planets, signs, and places of the zodiac, we look to the aspects, or configurations, as they're known in Hellenistic astrology, to establish the relationship between the celestial bodies in the zodiac chart. In the next chapter, we will introduce an additional layer to our cosmic understanding of movement through the zodiac: the relationships between the signs as they connect or disconnect from one another and the places (houses) in which they are embedded.

CHAPTER 6

Aspects and Configurations

In Hellenistic astrology, the harmonious or disharmonious relationships between planets are recognized by five configurations, known in modern astrology as aspects. The conditions are determined by the seven visual rays shown from the planet of origin. These seven visual rays reflect a "beam of light" so that the planet of origin can "see" or "bear witness" to the other placements in the chart.

This witnessing can be a loving, nurturing gaze or a vindictive, evil one. Among these seven rays, three move upward toward the Southern Hemisphere, three shoot downward toward the Northern Hemisphere, and the last shoots straight across to the other side of the chart. The six rays that shoot upward and downward are divided into three categories of two: the nearest two rays from the planet in question are sextile or 60 degrees away, ruled by Venus. The next two rays are square or 90 degrees away from the planet, ruled by Mars. Two more rays are trine or 120 degrees away, ruled by Jupiter. The seventh ray is in diameter or opposition from the planet in question, facing directly across the chart, and is ruled by Saturn.

In this section, we will go deeper into understanding the five configurations and the relationships they have with one another.

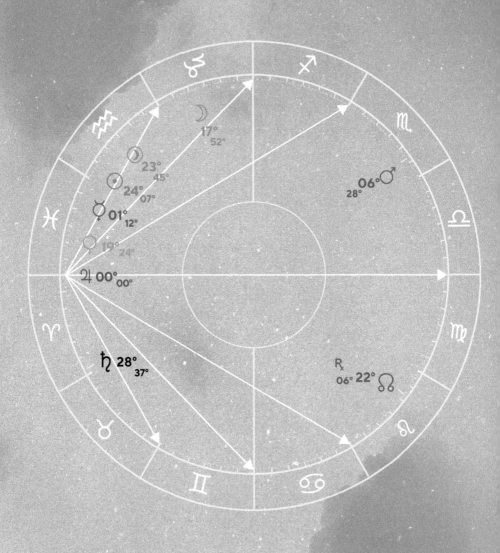

ASPECT	DEGREES	PLACEMENT	RELATIONSHIP	PLANETARY RULER
Conjunction (Copresence)	**0** degrees	Close connection between placements	Placements have a strong influence on each other, either harmonious or disharmonious.	None; possibly the Sun and Moon
Hexagon (Sextile)	**60** degrees	Separated by two signs apart	Pleasant but has no "help" from the aspecting placement.	Venus
Tetragon (Square)	**90** degrees	Separated by three signs apart	Placements are at cross purposes and may result in frustration or tension.	Mars
Triangle (Trine)	**120** degrees	Separated by four signs apart	The most positive connection. The placements offer each other support through action.	Jupiter
Diameter (Opposition)	**180** degrees	Separated by six signs apart	Placements are parallel but moving in opposite directions; they have different motivations.	Saturn

The Five Configurations

Antiochus and Porphyry defined and unpacked the astrological concept of aspects or configurations (*schemastismos*) within the chart by using both sign-based and degree-based configurations and by using a connection with a planet in the same sign or the same degree (which will be discussed later on in this chapter). The ancient Greek word *schemastismos* can be further broken down to the word *scheme*, which means a form, shape, or geometric figure.

These geometric schemes or figures are represented by the five original configurations in the chart: the tetragon or square, the triangle or trine, the hexagon or sextile, the diameter or opposition, and the conjunction. The connection between these configurations are also determined by their qualities, namely gender, triplicity, quadruplicity, exaltation, and their benefic or malefic status. We will go into more detail to determine what these geometric configurations mean to the relationship of the placements.

CONJUNCTION (COPRESENCE)

The fifth configuration is the conjunction, or copresence (*sumparousia*). The conjunction was originally excluded from the seven visual rays, or the four proper configurations. This was because the placements involved, either in the same degree, planet, or sign, were not "witnessing" or looking at each other but, instead, were present together or in each other's company.

When placements are "with each other" or conjunct, they have a strong influence over each other. When the placements of a conjunction are exact, or under 4 degrees of arc of distance, it can be like two cymbals being struck simultaneously. It will be difficult to decipher the two sounds from each other. Having a conjunction is a strong aspect, in which the individual might not be aware of their own energy, but this energy can be felt strongly by others.

Someone with a conjunction will think that others feel similarly to them when in fact, unless those others also have a conjunction, they will not be able to understand what this person experiences. It is like having a mark on your face that others can see, but you can only see it with a mirror to know that it is there.

The conjunction is at 0 degrees. In numerology, the number zero represents the energy of all or nothing. It defines the whole as well as the infinite. The energy of zero can denote a positive inclination, giving an individual the perception that they have the power to overcome challenges or to believe that anything is possible. Zero can also create an idealized delusion in the native, giving them a mistaken sense of reality or an absence of connection.

In astrology, this reveals a "blending together" effect or an added "intensity" of the placements. If Mars is conjunct the Ascendant, the qualities of the planet are also added to the perceived outlook. The individual with Mars conjunct a Libra Ascendant can come across as aggressive, nonconforming, or threatening at times, even though the nature of the Libra sign is one of balance and pleasantness.

HEXAGON (SEXTILE)

The hexagon, or sextile, lies at 60 degrees from the placement of origin in the chart. Sextiles are associated with complementary elements or signs, so Air signs will sextile Fire signs and Water signs will sextile Earth signs.

For instance, Gemini and Leo are both expressive, popular, and bold, so a sextile will result in a positive connection. This can result in an amplification of each sign's positive qualities, so an individual will be extra sparkling and witty, if they work at it.

The sextile aspect provides some tension, but only enough to coax one into change or growth. However, this positive tension is not as easily handed to them as it is with the trine or made almost impossible with the square or opposition. The sextile is connected to the number six and the planet Venus, where harmony, pleasure, enjoyment, and connection can occur, but only with a push from other aspects. There must be a determination of value and worth.

With the sextile, we possess the potential for talents and abilities but need to put in the work for them to be actualized in our lives.

TETRAGON (SQUARE)

The tetragon, or square, at 90 degrees is a harsh configuration to have in one's chart. The square is represented by Mars in the Thema Mundi (page 48), bringing the malefic nature of this planet to every aspect that it touches.

A square in one's chart creates a relationship of intensity, power struggles, competition, fighting, and clashing energies. Unlike a diameter or opposition, the square occurs between discordant or disharmonious placements that are already in a tension-filled relationship.

Planets or signs with square placements work differently but also want different things, like a parent who wants to go home and rest and a toddler who wants to play and run around. They will have a hard time agreeing, especially if the parent is tired and the toddler is restless, and this will most likely create tension.

Too much tension can cause one to live in a heightened state of anxiety or exhaustion, whereas insufficient tension will fail to create growth or movement. The number four is about creating structure, discipline, and manifestation. With a square, we are meant to ascertain what structure needs to be created in order to release tension.

When we have fixed signs (Aquarius, Leo, Taurus, or Scorpio) as well as malefic planets (Mars and Saturn) involved in a square, the results can be powerful. The motivating energy of the square is used to engage in productive pursuits, which are those most likely represented by the more helpful aspects in our charts, like a sextile or a trine. This will move the focus from the negative and into the positive.

TRIANGLE (TRINE)

The triangle, or trine, at 120 degrees, was said by Porphyry to be "sympathetic and helpful, and even if a destructive star is there, it is less damaging." The trine is represented by Jupiter, the great benefic, in the Thema Mundi, making it the most positive aspect in the group of the five configurations. This "soft" or pleasant aspect is said to represent luck, happiness, and a natural talent or skill. This natural skill or ability may be something that we are not even aware we possess.

Trines are normally seen among signs of the same element or triplicity: Air, Fire, Water, or Earth. For example, a placement in Aries can only be in trine with the other Fire signs, Sagittarius and Leo. Trines can also be between planets in different signs, such as Jupiter in Aries trine Moon in Leo. The aspects support and do not restrict each other.

The trine is a place of ease, friendship, and harmony, quite possibly a reward from a previous life. It shows us what we like, what we excel at, and what people like about us. An individual with a trine in their chart does not need to do much or create new structures in order to benefit from this aspect.

Just as Jupiter can represent many good things, good karma, and good relationships, it can also represent too much of a good thing. The trine can sometimes be taken for granted or overlooked by some individuals who have this aspect. The trine can produce ease and healing but not growth. These happen with challenge, and if there is no challenge, there is no growth.

DIAMETER (OPPOSITION)

The diameter, or opposition, at 180 degrees, is regarded by Brennan as "the most difficult configuration of the literature" in Hellenistic astrology. The opposition can create tension just by having an opposing sign in the chart. This is because the opposing sign, place, or degree is always the opposite of the placement in question. This opposition naturally creates tension because the two involved placements do not see eye to eye, are always operating in different directions, and, like parallel lines, will never meet or agree.

The opposition is a relationship of tension, challenges, battles, extremes, and rivalry. The placements want similar but different things, like having the doorbell ring at both the front and back doors at the same time—which one do you answer first? Oppositions represent signs such as Leo-Aquarius, Libra-Aries, Taurus-Scorpio, Gemini-Sagittarius, Cancer-Capricorn, and Virgo-Pisces.

This aspect relates to the number two, which represents duality or confusion. This can sometimes manifest as an inner battle within the individual, as they will be "of two minds" or have opposing ways of thinking or operating in the world.

OPPOSITES ATTRACT?

The diameter or opposition in the Thema Mundi is associated with Saturn, itself a malefic planet, as it is opposed to the Cancer ascendant in the Hour-Marker place as well as the Moon in Cancer. In the Thema Mundi, Saturn forms a natural opposition of 180 degrees to the Moon.

Porphyry notes that the "diameter is adversarial, but worse if a malefic star is present." In life, some say that opposites attract, but in astrology, they can bring out the worst qualities in each other because they are so very different. Both oppositional signs are operating on different wavelengths that confuse and possibly antagonize each other.

The aforementioned individual will struggle with expressing themself in a calm manner. Saturn, the ruler of the opposition and a malefic, and Aries, a masculine sign, will be the more dominant force over Mercury, a neutral planet and one who will adhere to the strongest force present and will dominate Libra, a feminine, receptive sign.

Sign-Based Configurations

Sign-based configurations, or aspects, occur when planets are in a sign that is configured to be able to recognize another sign. If they are unable to recognize or "see each other," then they cannot relate to each other. Theophrastus, a Greek philosopher, notes that "the one party is persuaded by the thought that the other things are, for the most part, best interpreted by similarity; that is innate to all creatures who know their kin." Like attracts like. Sign-based configurations combine those signs that are in the same element or quadruplicity, quality or triplicity, and gender.

For instance, Cancer will associate well with Virgo, as they share the same gender and are sextile each other, and there is a pleasantness associated there. Cancer can also have a sign-based configuration with Scorpio, as they are both feminine Water signs. They will understand and attract each other. Similarly, two planets in the same sign can have a strong connection regardless of their location in the chart. This is called copresence. This energy of connection is called the quincunx or semi-sextile, also referred to as aversion (*apostrophe*).

AVERSION

A set of placements in aversion or quincunx are "turned away" or "unconnected" (*asundetos*) from each other, but even though they are unable to see each other on the chart, they can still help each other. These signs are coming from completely different directions and can offer very different skills that they may not be aware of in each other.

For instance, Aquarius is semi-sextile or in aversion to Sagittarius because on the chart, they are not in each other's line of sight. Capricorn is in between them, blocking their view. Still, they are able to offer gifts to each other that the other may be lacking. Aquarius can provide Sagittarius with the ability to think through their actions before moving. Sagittarius can bring a sense of motivation and positivity to Aquarius. The individual with this birth chart may also not be able to connect with lost qualities that they cannot "see." They may have trouble thinking things through or being very positive.

Unlike squares and oppositions, the quincunx is a more subtle energy. A square or opposition might show up as a recent breakup or a loss of a job, whereas the quincunx might be a roomful of laundry that needs to be done. All of these can be difficult to deal with, but the breakup and the job loss are "louder" in comparison to the dirty laundry. The laundry sometimes takes a back seat to this individual's being able to provide for themself. In the front seat would be the need to find a new job or to deal with the emotional stress of someone they love leaving their life.

COPRESENCE

A copresence is like a conjunction in that planets of the same sign, house, or place exist together, like roommates living in the same apartment. They may be very different energies and might operate in various ways, but they will begin to influence each other over time because they are sharing the same place or sign.

In the Thema Mundi, there is a copresence in the first place. Cancer on the Ascendant and the Moon in Cancer in the first house represent a sign-based conjunction. Signs or planets do not have to be directly next to each other to possess a strong influence.

If someone's chart has Jupiter in Virgo at 2 degrees and Mars in Virgo at 28 degrees, those planets still share the same Virgoan qualities even though they are very far apart and not conjunct. The person may be extra fastidious or critical, as there is a strong dose of Virgo in the conjunction or copresence.

THE REVIVAL OF TRADITIONAL ASTROLOGY IN THE MODERN ERA

As discussed in previous chapters, the transmission of astro-logical techniques was not a smooth one. Astrology suffered the imposition of Christianity, the internal conflict between astrology and astronomy as subjects of scientific study, invasions from other cultures like the Goths, and the eventual movement of astrology into an "underground science."

Astrologers in the 1980s began to connect modern astrology to Hellenistic astrology. James Herschel Holden translated many traditional Arabic and Latin texts, such as Abu Ali al-Khayyat's *Book of Nativities*, a text from the ninth century. Robert Zoller revisited Hellenistic astrology in his *The Lost Key to Prediction: The Arabic Parts in Astrology*.

Similar to the Spiritualism movement in 19th-century England, which connected astrology with the supernatural, astrologers in the 1990s began to connect the science of astrology with psychology. The basic idea was that a person can project the past and the inner workings of their sub-conscious mind onto the environment and their birth chart. With this, modern astrologers moved away from the fatalis-tic notion surrounding traditional astrology and embraced a more humanistic, spiritual, and psychological basis to their astrological readings.

Degree-Based Configurations

The degree-based configurations determine where the ray of light shines from the planet or placement of origin to the following energies. There is an energy of scrutiny or "observation" (*katopteuo*) between the placement of origin and where the light comes to rest.

For instance, if the Sun is in Leo in the second place at 16 degrees, it will shine two sextile rays of 16 degrees to Libra in the fourth place and to Gemini in the twelfth place. The Sun will shine two square rays of 16 degrees to Scorpio in the fifth place and Taurus in the eleventh place. Lastly, the Sun will shine two 16-degree rays to Sagittarius in the sixth place and to Aries in the tenth place. The Sun will also shine a ray for an opposition of 16 degrees in Aquarius.

The visual ray has the strongest energy at the point of 16 degrees within each placement. A degree-sign configuration can occur when two planets or placements are at exactly 60, 90, 120, or 180 degrees away from each other. For instance, a Sun in Cancer at 10 degrees will have a degree-based configuration to the Moon in Taurus at ten degrees. Even though they are already sextile by sign to each other, the degree-based configuration is stronger than if, say, the Moon was in Taurus at 17 degrees.

APPLYING VERSUS SEPARATING

Applying or joining (*sunaphe*) and separating or flowing away (*aporroia*) adheres to the idea that an aspect can be applied to a configuration within 3 and 15 degrees of their conjunction (applying) and within 1 degree (separation). This holds true regardless of whether the planets are in direct or indirect (retrograde) motion, which according to Antiochus is called the "assembly" (*sunodos*). These assembly applications of degree consideration are akin to the use of orbs in modern astrology. The speed of the planets is also a factor in determining application or separation.

The planets from slowest to fastest are Pluto, Neptune, Uranus, Saturn, Jupiter, Mars, the Sun, Venus, Mercury, and the Moon, denoting the relationship from the teacher, Pluto, all the way to the student, the Moon. Moving in a counterclockwise fashion around the chart, in an application, the faster of the two planets is seen as the "active" or superior force, the one causing the commotion and moving rapidly toward the slower or "inferior" planet. In a separation, the faster or superior planet is moving away from the slower, inferior planet.

There is also a factor of the left (*euonumos*) and right (*dexios*) sides of the chart and where the planets are in this right/left dictum, which is marked by the straight line of opposition or diameter across the chart. The right side holds the energy of the planet that has just moved away, increasing its distance, and the left side holds the planets that the planet of origin is moving toward, decreasing its distance.

The faster planet is always learning from the slower planets. Consider, for example, Venus in Aries at 10 degrees in opposition to Pluto in Libra at 7 degrees. Venus is faster and closer to the Sun, so it is learning a lesson from Pluto, which is a very slow, outer planet. As the planets come closer together by degree, you can feel the energy coming closer and know that something is about to happen. When applying this to a chart, it is the impending feeling that an emotional or dramatic collision will occur in your life, such as a bankruptcy or birth of a child.

The separating occurrence can feel like a relief, such as paying off student loan debt or finally landing a new job after months of applying. You will feel relieved after a separating aspect and nervous or in flux with an applying aspect.

In this chapter, we were able to determine the configurations or aspects that establish key relationships between the planets and signs in the birth chart. Now, in the next chapter, we will bring all of these ideas together and explore the time-lord techniques used in Hellenistic astrology, including annual profections and zodiacal releasing, which will help us determine key events in the life of an individual.

CHAPTER 7

Bringing It All Together

In this section, we will tie together all the methods, theories, and practices discussed throughout the book to develop a complete understanding of Hellenistic birth chart interpretation.

We began the book by looking at the three different branches of Hellenistic astrology: natal (the study of the chart at birth), universal (the collective planetary energies), and katarchic (the use of astrology to pinpoint events like death or marriage).

We then examined the seven wandering stars (the Sun, the Moon, Saturn, Mars, Jupiter, Mercury, and Venus). We also looked at the two sects (diurnal and nocturnal), the qualities of placements (such as the gender, triplicity, quadruplicity, exaltations, and depressions), the morning and evening stars, the lots, and the speed and stations of the planets.

From there, we were able to understand the ecliptic and its division into the twelve equal parts or signs and twelve places. Lastly, we learned about the configurations, or aspects, and how they connect the energies of the celestial bodies.

In modern astrology, we use transits, the movement of the planets over the static natal chart, to determine changes in the individual horoscope. With Hellenistic astrology, we can determine key events in an individual's life.

Time-Lord Techniques

Similar to the Dasha system in Vedic astrology, the time-lord techniques are a method to make predictions and track changes in the astrological chart. This was practiced from about 200 BCE to 700 CE. Many of the original time-lord techniques were lost as techniques related to Hellenistic astrology were transposed and transferred to India and parts of Europe.

Though modern astrologers prefer to use the transit system, which evaluates the passing of moving planets across the stationary snapshot of a birth chart, the time-lord techniques are a method of monitoring changes in someone's life and the impact that these changes will have on the individual.

Transits are seen as a negotiated series of passing influences in one's chart, whereas time-lords have a more predestined determination—the actuality of fate versus the determination of will.

The time-lord techniques are based on the self-activation of a planet, place, or house within the zodiac chart that determines when events will happen in an individual's life, the timing of which changes from person to person. An activation of a placement can occur for many reasons, namely major phases in a person's life, such as going through puberty or moving into adulthood. The placement has a specific time when it is set to "light up" or become activated in the inner and outer lives of the native. Brennan adds that these techniques are based on the "division of the times, because they are usually designed to divide up the native's life into different chapters and subsections, each possessing different qualities and characteristics." Time-lords operate in shifts rather than occurring all at once. Certain placements can lie dormant in someone's chart for years while the individual feels no connection to the energy of that planet or place. Suddenly, they can emerge, and the latent potential of this placement may be realized in the life of the person.

It is said that this is a karmic placement, which unfolds of its own judgment and accord. By using time-lord techniques, we see when these occurrences will impact the individual's life. When a planet has a time-lord, it allows only the matters, themes, or subjects of that time-lord to happen at that particular time. There are a few major systems used to work with the time-lord in astrology, but in Hellenistic astrology, the most widespread methods are annual profections and zodiacal releasing.

TIMING AND TRANSITS

The time-lord techniques in Hellenistic astrology are very similar to the transit system used in modern astrology today. In the time-lord methods, each planet has a sort of timer for when it is set to "go off" and self-activate in the life of an individual. This activation stimulates challenges, or growth, in which the individual is transitioning into a new frame of mind, either internally with their belief systems or externally with the loss of a job or natural disaster.

The transit system works in a similar way, but we start by looking at the transits of the individual planets in relation to that particular individual, starting with the outer planets first (Saturn, Pluto, Uranus, and Neptune), as they take longer to orbit someone's chart and have a longer-lasting effect. Next we look at the placement of the Moon, which cycles and changes signs every two and a half days. Then we look at Mars, which takes about two years to cycle through the whole zodiac, activating the "energy/boredom" cycle. As Mars moves closer to your natal Mars sign, it increases your energy, and as it moves away, it decreases your energy.

Annual Profections

Annual profections are the most used Hellenistic time-lord system to organize and prioritize which transits, or shifts, in one's chart are the most important in a given year. A planet could not be activated unless the time was right and it was ready to be "seen" in the native's chart.

Thus, profections "advance" or move the chart along starting from the Ascendant, the beginning of identity and persona, to the other planets and placements. The time-lord would exist within any planet that received a profection, namely the traditional rulers of the signs and placements, the seven celestial bodies (excluding Uranus, Neptune, and Pluto).

The system can only work within the whole-house sign system, as one place is ruled by a particular sign, and it follows on in order of the places or houses. So if the first place, the Hour-Marker, has Virgo as its Ascendant, the second place or house would be Libra, the third place or house would hold Scorpio, and so on.

Brennan details the best method for calculating an annual profection: "Beginning with the rising sign, count one sign per year from that sign in zodiacal order for every year of the native's life. Whatever sign is reached in a given year; the domicile lord of that sign becomes activated as the time-lord for the year."

For instance, if an individual has Libra on the Ascendant, then the domicile lord, Venus, would be activated, and this will last from birth until they are one year old. When the person turns one, the next sign on the planetary list is Scorpio, and the domicile lord Mars (not Pluto) would be activated until they are two years old. In time, this chain of events, or profection, will make its way around the person's zodiac.

At 12, the process would begin again, with Venus once again becoming activated in the native's chart. The profection of the Ascendant is activated in 12-year cycles, starting at 0, then 12, 24, 36, and 48, continuing in increments of 12 from that point onward.

When using an annual profection chart, an astrologer would count forward starting from the Ascendant at zero, moving counterclockwise until it returned back to the Ascendant, which would be referred to as 12, then again counting in a counterclockwise manner until they returned to the Ascendant again, which would be 24. This will carry on to the outer sections of the annual profection chart.

ANALYZING ANNUAL PROFECTIONS
IN A BIRTH CHART

Annual profections are analyzed to determine key points in an individual's life. The topic or theme ruling the energy of that house or place has dominion over the individual for that year.

For instance, if a profection occurs at the sixth place, the individual might be confronted with issues related to illness, work ethic, their day-to-day jobs or routines, and general health concerns. A profection in the seventh place will have jurisdiction over relationships, partnerships, love, and business matters. A way of referring to the activated area is using the activated place and referencing the year, such as "sixth place profection year" or "seventh place profection year" and so on.

The planet ruling the sign in that place plays a large role in determining the condition of the year and whether it will be one of pain and discomfort, one of growth and expansion, or one of abundance and luck. If the lord of the year is well situated, it will result in a prosperous or positive year, but if malefic connections occur, then this will not be the case. One must understand the condition of the planet, the triplicities, quadruplicities, gender, sect, and so on to determine if it will bring joy or pain for the native.

For instance, a sixth profection year in Aries would have Mars as the lord of the year. Mars is a malefic planet in a malefic place, the sixth, so the native will need to be careful with health matters and their workplace.

The figure on page 112 is the birth chart of actor Tom Hanks, born July 9, 1956, at 11:17 a.m. in Concord, California. We notice that his first place profection year is in the sign of Virgo with a ruling planet of Mercury. Mercury is seen as the profection ruler from birth to the first year of his life, then Libra and Venus the second year, Scorpio and Mars the third year, up until Virgo and Mercury again become the profection when he is twelve.

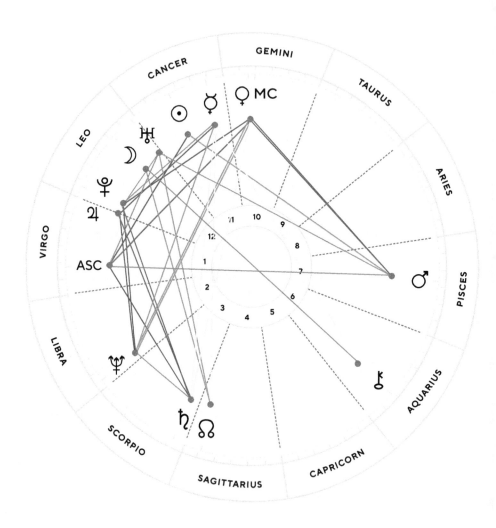

Hanks has a diurnal chart—the Southern Hemisphere rules his public persona from the seventh through the twelfth houses, so anything in these houses would already be illuminated. The majority of his astrological placements are in this hemisphere, allowing him to be more in the public eye than normal. An examination of Hanks's film career shows that his first major mainstream movie, *Big*, was released in 1988, when Hanks was 32, meaning that the profection landed in his ninth place of Taurus.

There are no planets in the ninth place, so we will move to the energy of that place. The ninth place is the place of foreign travel, foreigners, and the house of God. Anything in this place will be elevated to a godlike status; in that vein, *Big* was his first international box-office hit, the film that catapulted him into stardom. In addition, Taurus is a fixed feminine sign ruled by Venus, so Venus becomes the time-lord of his ninth place, a benefic placement. He is seen as magnanimous on screen, but not in a dominating way, more in a loveable, endearing, and accessible way.

His Jupiter is also sextile his Neptune, also in Libra, doubling the positive Venusian energy held by Hanks during this movie. Venus has bestowed upon him charisma and charm in order to captivate an audience.

The figure on page 114 is the birth chart of Barack Obama, the 44th president of the United States, born August 4, 1961, at 7:24 p.m. in Honolulu, Hawaii. Obama has a nocturnal chart, so the Moon and the sect belonging to the Moon—Venus, Jupiter, Mars, and Saturn—have a benefic effect in this chart. The nocturnal sect placements play a large role in the positive occurrences in Obama's chart.

In October 1992, at the age of 31, he was experiencing a ninth place profection year in Virgo when he married his wife, Michelle. Mars, normally a malefic planet, resides in this place, but because his chart is nocturnal, this has become a more positive influence and most likely prompted him to step further into his passions and determine the place of God within his life.

This coincided with his reelection to the Illinois Senate in May 2002 while reassessing his presidential prospects the same year,

✳ BARACK OBAMA • August 4, 1961 • 7:24pm

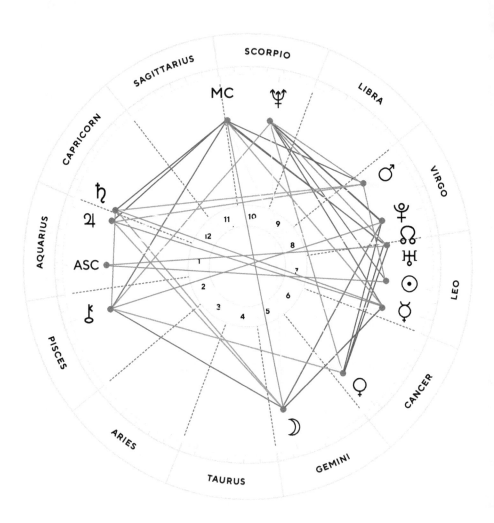

which culminated with his election to the US Senate in 2005, and then motivating his bid for the White House. Of course, it is possible that Michelle was a motivating or at least positive factor in this decision.

When he was inaugurated as president of the United States on January 20, 2009, at the age of 48, he was experiencing a first place profection year in Aquarius with the planet Jupiter at the Helm. Jupiter, already a benefic planet, was made doubly so by being placed in the house of Obama's Ascendant. Jupiter is sextile his Midheaven in the tenth place of Scorpio. Mars in Virgo is trine his Jupiter in Aquarius, which are all positive aspects. Jupiter is activated by the profection and motivated him to move forward on his career path and have stronger public focus, engaging the Midheaven.

ASTROLOGY, FATE, FORTUNE, AND LUCK

Would someone want to know when they are going to die or when their lover will leave them? Maybe most of us would like to know when or if we will have children or feel comfortable monetarily. Deciphering the lots is key to understanding these concepts, encapsulating the idea of fate and fortune, destiny and free will.

The focus on good fortune was not taken lightly by Hellenistic astrologers. A key way to determine one's fortune is by looking at the planetary rulers and places in residence as close as possible to the Midheaven, the apex of our chart in the Southern Hemisphere, our key to happiness in our careers and professional lives. Using time-lord techniques like annual profections and zodiacal releasing can give us an indication of which planet, either malefic or benefic, is "ruling over" the life of an individual at that particular point.

Zodiacal Releasing

Vettius Valens referred to zodiacal releasing, or *aphesis*, as one of the most powerful and accurate time-lord techniques. The ancient Greek term *aphesis* means "letting go," "release," or "dismissal." The person is able to "release" the energy associated with a certain sign or planet according to a timed set of years in their chart.

This method is similar to the annual profection technique in that it determines key aspects in an individual's life, but it differs in that it can record along decades and can divide the native's life into "chapters or paragraphs," the most important of which are key topics like health, love, and one's career. Modern astrologers, like Brennan and George, believe that this technique gives the most accurate assessments of timing and major life occurrences in one's chart.

Unlike annual profections, the starting points to determine the key time periods in an individual's life with zodiacal releasing are the Lot of Spirit and the Lot of Fortune. Astrologers would release from the Lot of Spirit for matters relating to the mind, career, and life direction. They would then release from the Lot of Fortune for matters related to the body, health, and illnesses.

Once the lot is chosen based on the matter, consider that each sign is given a certain amount of time as based on the number of years attributed to its domicile lord. There are minor planetary periods ascribed to the seven celestial bodies: the Sun at 19 years, the Moon at 25 years, Saturn at 30 years, Mercury at 20 years, Venus at 8 years, Mars at 15 years, and Jupiter at 12 years.

The signs and their attributed years for zodiacal releasing are Leo at 19 years, Cancer at 25 years, Capricorn at 27 years (even though Saturn has 30 years), Virgo and Gemini at 20 years, Libra and Taurus at 8 years, Aries and Scorpio at 15 years, and Sagittarius and Pisces at 12 years.

The zodiacal releasing chart uses 360 days with 30 days each month so that each month encompasses exactly one-twelfth of a year, making twelve months in a year, completely even. The chart is divided into four levels: "years," "months," "weeks," and "days," each of which moves at different speeds around the zodiac, with each level as one-twelfth of the duration of the level above it.

Level 1 is the general period showing the "years" within a 360-day period. Level 2 is the first subperiod showing the "months" within a 30-day period. Level 3 is the second subperiod of "weeks" in a 2½-day period. Lastly, Level 4 is the third subperiod in "days" in a 5-hour period.

To ascertain the quality of the placement in zodiacal releasing, one should look at the qualities and position of the activated sign along with the qualities of the natal planet of that sign. One would start the process with the place where the Lot of Spirit is located and then count counterclockwise through the signs until one reaches one of the angles of Fortune (as discussed in the following paragraph), which represent moments of heightened activity and importance in the individual's life.

The ranking of angles follows the ranking of the places utilized in a Hellenistic astrology practice—this shows that the first and tenth signs relative to the Lot of Fortune are the most important and prominent signs. The next most powerful is the seventh sign from the Lot of Fortune, also called the "moderate peak period." Next, the fourth sign from the Lot of Fortune is also referred to as the "minor peak period."

As not everyone will have an interaction with a peak angle, the general period can represent strong, life-changing activity for the individual. Regardless of whether you start with the Lot of Fortune or the Lot of Spirit, the first sign or lot represented is under the jurisdiction of those particular years allotted to the planet it rules over.

For example, if you wanted to study the person's health, you would look to the Lot of Fortune. If this lot begins with Aries, then for a person born in 1980, the allotted years are 15. So from 0 to 15 years of age (from 1980 to 1995), the individual is ruled by Arian energy within their health factor. Due to Aries' malefic and masculine nature, this person might have health issues due to accidents or injuries to the head or face.

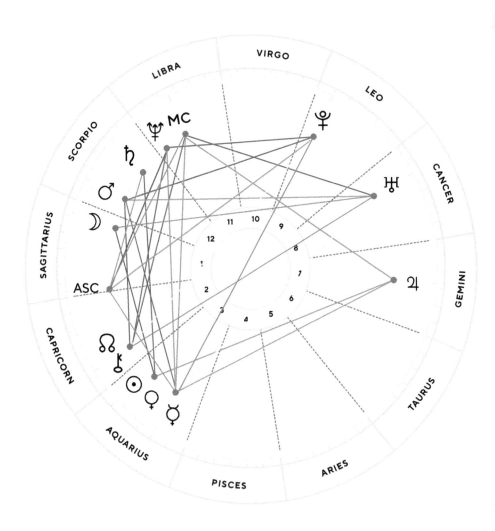

ANALYZING ZODIACAL RELEASING
IN A BIRTH CHART

Below, we will look at and dissect the birth charts of two popular celebrities, Oprah Winfrey and Michael J. Fox, using the zodiacal releasing method.

The figure on page 118 is the birth chart of Oprah Winfrey, born January 29, 1954, at 4:30 a.m., in Kosciusko, Mississippi. In this instance, we are only interested in looking at her Lot of Spirit, which rules the Sun and the mind, in order to look into her career.

To calculate the Lot of Spirit, we use the formula Day: Moon - Sun + Ascendant = Lot of Spirit (diurnal), as her chart is a morning chart. So, we start with her Moon in Sagittarius at 4, 31 degrees in the first place, after which we move to the Sun in Aquarius at 8, 59 degrees in the third place, returning a calculation of 64 degrees. We take the 64 degrees and apply it to her Ascendant and, measuring 64 degrees from that point in a clockwise position, we get a Lot of Spirit of Libra in the eleventh place.

She starts off in a Venus-Libra period, which lasts 8 years from 0 to 7 years of age (or, from January 29, 1954, to December 18, 1961), so she is in a period of beauty, attraction, and connection with the mother. The next 15 years are marked with trauma and abuse as shown through the movement into Mars-Scorpio, which is also in the twelfth place, a place in decline ruled by Saturn, a malefic planet, showing discord, abuse, punishment, maltreatment, deceit, secrets, depression, and sorrow. This time would correlate with allegations of abuse during her childhood and teenage years (December 18, 1961, to September 30, 1976) at the hands of men in her town.

A period of prosperity happens in her career as she moves into the next sign of Sagittarius-Jupiter from September 30, 1976, to July 29, 1988, which coincides with her hosting a morning TV talk show in Chicago, where she also began the long-running *Oprah Winfrey Show*. During this time, she also starred in her first major movie, *The Color Purple*, in 1985. Jupiter bestowed her with "good

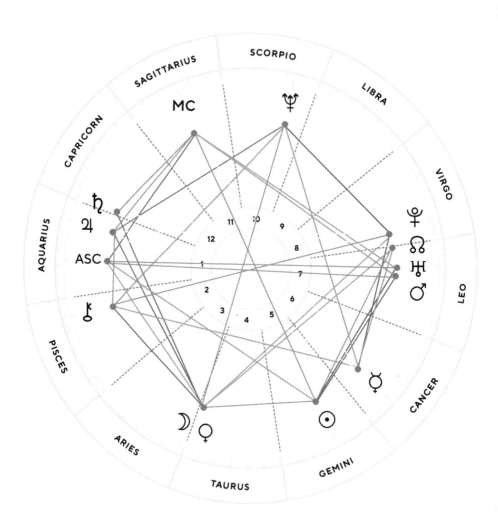

luck," recognition, abundance, a confirmation of good things and relief from bad things, freedom, and fellowship. Sagittarius is her first place, or the Helm, so this began the avalanche of opportunities that once forsook her. The longest time period of Capricorn-Saturn, in the second place from July 29, 1988, to March 10, 2015, is when she began to put down her Saturnian roots by becoming a producer, coinciding with the syndication of her TV show.

Now we will look at the birth chart for Michael J. Fox (page 120), born June 9, 1961, at 12:15 a.m. in Edmonton, Alberta, Canada. We'll examine the Lot of Fortune for a focus on his health and wellness.

To begin, we will use the calculation Day: Sun - Moon + Ascendant = Lot of Fortune (diurnal) for his day chart. His Lot of Fortune is in Aries, a masculine sign in his third place and a malefic. However, the Moon, the ruler of the nocturnal sect, is in this place as well, making it not as negative as it could have been. From June 9, 1961, to March 22, 1976, he loved sports and games but was not allowed to compete because of his short stature, so the malefic energy of the third place was neutralized by the presence of the Moon, the lord of the third place. He began acting while in his Taurus-Venus release (March 22, 1976, to February 9, 1984), which in the fourth house, one of the peak angles, represents a pivotal moment in his life when he landed the roles of Michael Keaton in *Family Ties* and Marty McFly in *Back to the Future*, which cemented his acting chops and pull in Hollywood.

From February 9, 1984, to October 27, 2003, during his Mercury-Gemini release, he was diagnosed with Parkinson's disease and took a hiatus from acting. Mercury rules hearing, versatility, and critical thinking, but as a neutral planet, it can bring about all of the misfortunes represented in our charts, especially if aspected by a malefic, with his Mercury sextile Pluto. The Mars energy of Pluto "dominated" his chart, and that planet brings "that which is hard and abrupt," pain, violence, falling down, blood, and poor vision. However, the Sun, also in this place, rules the head, heart, life breath, the nerves, and sensory movement. So the implantation of Mars in the energy of this release could have contributed to the sudden and violent turn that his health took in regard to his Parkinson's diagnosis.

Tools and Resources for Interpreting Your Chart

Casting your own Hellenistic chart can be a fun and eye-opening experience, especially if you are accustomed to completing an astrology chart using modern methods. I, for one, love working with secondary progressed charts and transits to determine key life moments in an individual's chart, and I find that the use of annual profections and zodiacal releasing has offered an additional level of depth and accuracy when pinpointing key happenings in a chart.

The ability to pinpoint key themes in an individual's chart is indispensable. As Brennan notes in his book *Hellenistic Astrology*, there are ethical and moral considerations that need to be respected when giving crucial information to an individual. Do we report a major illness or life-changing phenomenon that might produce anxiety or tension in the individual? This is the age-old dilemma with astrologers and diviners.

As most of chart construction is a manual and mathematics-based field, a wonderful resource for "checking your work" is Astro-Seek.com, which allows you to check profections, the Lots of Fortune and Spirit, and zodiacal releasing through a calculated computer system. This site should be utilized as a checker after you have completed or at least tried to work on finding the placements and configurations yourself.

Another wonderful site with informative and modern interpretations of astrology is the Astrology Institute. Run by astrologer Joseph Crane—a Buddhist, neurofeedback clinician, existential psychotherapist, and lecturer on mythology, literature, philosophy, and ancient and modern astrology—this website gives a thorough and analytical understanding of placements from both a modern and traditional viewpoint.

Understanding how to compute and study annual profections and zodiacal releasing adds to a deeper understanding of an individual's chart, offering a profound interpretation of key moments in an individual's life, through either their health or their career. In our final section, we will close this book with a last few notes and key takeaways from our discussion on Hellenistic astrology.

CHAPTER 8

Final Notes

Hellenistic astrology is a wonderful complement to modern astrology. This traditional practice answers key questions that many modern astrologers can sometimes take for granted.

Hellenistic astrology provides a deep understanding of the natural characteristics of planets, signs, and aspects that one would have difficulty comprehending without a thorough analysis of the mythology, history, and mathematical properties of these facets of the chart. Apart from this book, another goal of mine would be to write additional interpretations of these time-honored but often complicated practices and techniques and to offer a simplified version of traditional and professional texts.

Many of the practices in Hellenistic astrology, like annual profections and other time-lord techniques, are not utilized in modern astrology, and I feel that this a loss for the astrological community. By not only using transits, which do an amazing job of showing the natural progression of the zodiac signs and planets in a chart, but also using annual profections, one can specifically narrow in on time periods of interest, such as key career moves or changes, as shown in the interpretations of the charts of Oprah Winfrey and Michael J. Fox.

These key components could not be deciphered using modern astrology methods. One can ascertain an idea of what is to come but could not necessarily be able to point out to what extent, when, and why these actions are taking place, which traditional Hellenistic astrology techniques can do.

Moral responsibility also plays a role in chart analysis. Astrologers should be direct and straightforward with all clients and students, but as we are human beings and not computers or machines, we need to also exhibit a level of empathy and discernment when relaying challenging news or material from the past that may show up in the charts. The ideas of fate and free will are huge topics in the astrological community. A person might wonder, "What does it matter what I do? It is already decided for me!" Certainly, using the mathematical systems alone as created by ancient astrologers, operating in a cold, formulaic method, it would appear that way. It might seem that a person does not have control or agency over one's life—that it is already predetermined.

I believe that the answer is multifaceted. Exploring psychological and philosophical ideologies, such as determinism, stoicism, and rationalism, as well as divinatory practices and schools of thought, one would be able to establish their own personal values in regard to astrology and the ideas of fate versus free will. These are values that we all struggle with.

It is important for individual astrologers to have their own concept of these ideas to offer their clients and students. It is equally important for astrologers to provide for themselves continuity and connectedness to their own practice and sense of self. We use Hellenistic astrology not as a plea to go back to the traditional ways but as a way to inform ourselves of age-old, respected techniques that can be utilized today.

There is a special sense of continuity and wholeness in the realization that the sky our ancestors and early humans gazed upon is the same sky that we use today to connect with our pasts and futures. Using their techniques that worked to grant them answers and a relationship to nature and the gods, we are doing the same in the modern world.

The tools, techniques, and information that you procured in this book can enable you to connect to your past and future in a deeper way, where modern astrology sometimes seems to skim the surface. I would suggest that you reanalyze your chart using annual profections. Go back and think about the mythological connections of your astrological placements to the constellations and their stories of origin. See how much more you can discover about your astrological chart.

MORE READING

Hellenistic Astrology: The Study of Fate and Fortune by Chris Brennan

Astrology and the Authentic Self: Integrating Traditional and Modern Astrology to Uncover the Essence of the Birth Chart by Demetra George

A History of Horoscopic Astrology by James Herschel Holden

Aspects and House in Analysis by Noel Tyl

REFERENCES

Annus, Amar, ed. *Divination and Interpretation of Signs in the Ancient World*. Chicago: University of Chicago, 2010.

Antiochus. *The Thesaurus*. Translated by Robert H. Schmidt. Edited by Robert Hand. Berkeley Springs, WV: Golden Hind Press, 1993.

Arrian. *Anabasis of Alexander; or The History of the Wars and Conquests of Alexander the Great*. Translated by E. J. Chinnock. London: Hodder and Stoughton, 1884. Project Gutenberg. gutenberg.org /files/46976/46976-h/46976-h.htm.

Bauval, Robert. *The Egypt Code*. New York: Disinformation Company, 2008.

Brennan, Chris. *Hellenistic Astrology: The Study of Fate and Fortune*. Denver, CO: Amor Fati Publications, 2017.

Campion, Nicholas. *The Ancient World*. Vol. 1, *A History of Western Astrology*. New York: Continuum International Publishing Group, 2008.

Depuydt, Leo. "Ancient Egyptian Star Clocks and Their Theory." *Bibliotheca Orientalis* 55, no. 1 (1998): 6–44. doi.org/10.2143 /bior.55.1.2015844.

Dorotheus of Sidon. *Carmen Astrologicum: The First Book of Dorotheus from the Stars on the Judgements concerning Nativities on the Upbringing and Condition [of the Native]*. Translated by David Pingree. Leipzig: B. G. Teubner, 1976.

George, Demetra. *Assessing Planetary Condition*. Vol. 1, *Ancient Astrology in Theory and Practice: A Manual of Traditional Techniques*. Auckland, New Zealand: Rubedo Press, 2018.

George, Demetra. *Astrology and the Authentic Self: Integrating Traditional and Modern Astrology to Uncover the Essence of the Birth Chart*. Lake Worth, FL: Ibis Press, 2008.

Greenbaum, Dorian Gieseler. *The Daimon in Hellenistic Astrology: Origins and Influences*. Vol. 2. Edited by Tzvi Abusch, Ann K. Gulnan, Nils P. Heebel, Francesca Rochberg, and Frans A. M. Wiggerman. Boston: Brill Publications, 2016.

Haskell, Stephen N. *The Story of the Seer of Patmos*. Fort Worth, TX: Southern Publishing Association, 1905.

Hephaestion. *Apotelesmatics, Book II*. Translated by Robert H. Schmidt. Cumberland, MD: Golden Hind Press, 1998.

Holden, James Herschel. *A History of Horoscopic Astrology*. Tempe, AZ: American Federation of American Astrologers, 1996.

Irby-Massie, Georgia L., and Paul T. Keyser. *Greek Science of the Hellenistic Era: A Sourcebook*. London: Routledge, 2002.

Keyser, Paul T., and Georgia L. Irby-Massie, eds. *The Encyclopaedia of Ancient Natural Scientists*. London: Routledge, 2008.

Koch-Westenholz, Ulla. *Mesopotamian Astrology: An Introduction to Babylonian and Assyrian Celestial Divination*. Copenhagen, Denmark: Museum Tusculanum Press, 1995.

Manilius, Marcus. *Manili Astronomicon, Liber II*. Translated by Henry Frowde. Edited by H. W. Garrod. London: University of Oxford, 1911.

Maternus, Firmicus. *Ancient Astrology Theory and Practice: Matheseos Libri VIII*. Translated by Jean Rhys Bram. Park Ridge, NJ: Noyes Press, 1975.

Maternus, Firmicus. *Mathesis, or Ancient Astrology: Theory and Practice*. Translated by James H. Holden. Tempe, AZ: American Federation of American Astrologers, 2011.

Milton-Edwards, Beverley. "Iraq, Past, Present and Future: A Thoroughly-Modern Mandate?" History & Policy. May 8, 2003. historyandpolicy.org/policy-papers/papers/iraq-past-present -and-future-a-thoroughly-modern-mandate.

Oldfather, C. H., trans. *Diodorus of Sicily in Twelve Volumes, Books II, 35-IV, 58*. Vol. 2. Cambridge: Harvard University Press, 1935.

Pinch, Geraldine. *Magic in Ancient Egypt*. London: British Museum Press, 1994.

Pingree, David. *From Astral Omens to Astrology: From Babylon to Bikaner*. Rome: Liberia Distributions Degrassi, 1997.

Pliny. *Natural History*. Translated by Harris Rackham, William Henry Samuel Jones, and David Edward Eichholz. 10 vols. Cambridge: Harvard University Press, 1966–88.

Ptolemy, Claudius. *Tetrabiblos, Book I*. Translated by Robert Schmidt. Edited by Robert Hand. Berkeley Springs, WV: Golden Hind Press, 1994.

Ptolemy, Claudius. *Tetrabiblos, Book III*. Translated by Robert Schmidt. Edited by Robert Hand. Berkeley Springs, WV: Golden Hind Press, 1996.

Ptolemy, Claudius. *Tetrabiblos, Book IV*. Translated by Robert Schmidt. Edited by Robert Hand. Berkeley Springs, WV: Golden Hind Press, 1998.

Raphael. *A Manual of Astrology or the Book of the Stars: Being the Art of Fortune-Telling Future Events*. London: C. S. Arnold, 1828.

Rhetorius the Egyptian. *Astrological Compendium Containing His Explanation and Narration of the Whole Art of Astrology*. Translated by James Holden. Tempe, AZ: American Federation of Astrologers, 2009.

Rochberg, Francesca. *Babylonian Horoscopes*. Philadelphia: American Philosophical Society, 1998.

Sachs, Abraham J., and Hermann Hunger. *Astronomical Diaries and Related Texts from Babylonia*. Vienna: Verlag der Osterreichischen Akademie der wissenschaften, 1988.

Sextus Empiricus. *Against the Professors*. Translated by R. G. Bury. Cambridge: Harvard University Press, 1949.

Valens, Vettius. *Anthology, Book I*. Translated by James Herschel Holden. Tempe, AZ: American Federation of Astrologers, 1994.

Valens, Vettius. *Anthology, Book II*. Translated by Robert Schmidt. Berkeley Springs, WV: The Golden Hind Press, 1994.

Wardle, David. *Cicero on Divination*. Oxford: Clarendon Press, 2006.

Zoller, Robert. *The Lost Key to Prediction: The Arabic Parts in Astrology*. New York: Inner Traditions, 1980.

INDEX

ABOUT THE AUTHOR

Malorine Mathurin is a professional Hellenistic and Intuitive astrologer, energy healer, cartomancer, and clairvoyant. She enjoys the works of traditional texts from Vettius Valens and Manlius, as well as modern astrologers Noel Tyl, Dorian Gieseler Greenbaum, and Robert Hand. Malorine has a fine arts degree in painting and printmaking and art history and a research degree in cultural anthropology from the University of East Anglia, Norwich, UK, with a specialization in the arts and divination practices of Native American groups in the northeastern region of the United States. Malorine offers astrological workshops, Moon seminars, energy healing techniques, and one-on-one birth chart analysis using traditional Hellenistic techniques. She enjoys learning about astrology and divination throughout history, as well as painting, teaching, and collecting tarot card decks. Follow Malorine at MoonLadyAstrology.com.

CPSIA information can be obtained
at www.ICGtesting.com
Printed in the USA
JSHW041213070820
7156JS00002B/2